3

ignite English

Teacher Companion

Jill Carter
Christopher Edge
Peter Ellison
Liz Hanton
Mel Peeling
Alison Smith

Consultant
Geoff Barton

OXFORD

UNIVERSITY PRESS

OXFORD
UNIVERSITY PRESS

Great Clarendon Street, Oxford, OX2 6DP, United Kingdom

Oxford University Press is a department of the University of Oxford.
It furthers the University's objective of excellence in research, scholarship, and education
by publishing worldwide. Oxford is a registered trade mark of Oxford University Press in
the UK and in certain other countries

© Oxford University Press 2014

First published in 2014

British Library Cataloguing in Publication Data

Data available

978-0-19-839247-7

10 9 8 7 6 5 4 3 2

Paper used in the production of this book is a natural, recyclable product made from
wood grown in sustainable forests. The manufacturing process conforms to the
environmental regulations of the country of origin.

Printed in Great Britain by Bell and Bain Ltd., Glasgow

Page layout by Phoenix Photosetting.

MIX
Paper from
responsible sources
FSC
www.fsc.org   FSC® C007785

Contents

Ignite English has been written by people who love teaching English. It was a pre-requisite for us when developing this resource that you have people who are confident teaching English and who would find it patronizing to tell you how to teach English. Therefore we have provided a flexibility, both digitally and on the page, so that you can decide how you are going to customize it for your students.

In *Ignite English*, we also take English and show how it relates to the real world. Outside school there are lots of people doing lots of different jobs who will be using speaking, listening, reading and writing, and we might not even think about how they are doing it. Well let's! In *Ignite English*, we take a look at what they do and we talk to them about how they are doing it, so that you and your students can explore the way they are using language and connect what we are doing in the classroom with the world out there.

Informed by research and recent Ofsted reports, *Ignite English* aims to help reinvigorate KS3 English teaching and learning by:

- Improving learning through relevance and creativity
- Ensuring teaching is distinctive
- Enabling effective transition between Year 6 and Year 7
- Accessing up-to-date and relevant professional development
- Delivering the new KS3 National Curriculum

That is essentially what we are trying to do with *Ignite English*.

Geoff Barton

Series Consultant, Head Teacher, Teacher of English and highly experienced English author

Ignite English authors

Ignite English was created with Geoff Barton and authored by experienced teachers and educationalists who are passionate about teaching English. As well as being tested in schools and reviewed by teachers, the resources were also reviewed by Peter Ellison, a cross-phase Local Authority Adviser and Phil Jarrett, former Ofsted National Adviser for English.

Relevance

English as a subject covers all sorts of reading, writing and spoken English skills, texts and contexts. Our intention is to help students see the connections between what they are learning in English lessons in school and the world beyond the school gate.

So, in *Ignite English*, students will meet a range of people, from writers and actors through to business people and the military, whose jobs are linked thematically to the unit they are exploring. Many of the reading, writing and spoken English skills that students need every day are the skills they need to develop through their English lessons. *Ignite English* also aims to help students understand how they can apply the key English skills they are developing in real-world contexts.

Creativity

Being able to respond in a creative and personal way is a vital part of English lessons. *Ignite English* offers students a wide range of reading, writing and spoken English tasks that ask students to respond in lots of different and creative ways. From tweeting and texting to selecting winning texts for a competition to essays and reports, *Ignite English* aims to provide students with variety and opportunities for creativity.

Distinctiveness

Learning what students are good at and learning what they need to improve on are an essential part of English.

Each unit in *Ignite English* opens with a 'big question', which sits underneath all the learning that will happen throughout that unit. At appropriate points in each unit, students have opportunities to evaluate their progress and at the end of the unit they will have an assessment, often in a real-world context, which gives them the opportunity to show what they have learned.

All of these features aim to allow students to understand more about the texts and skills offered in English lessons, to discover what interests them and to express themselves clearly in relevant, creative and distinctive ways.

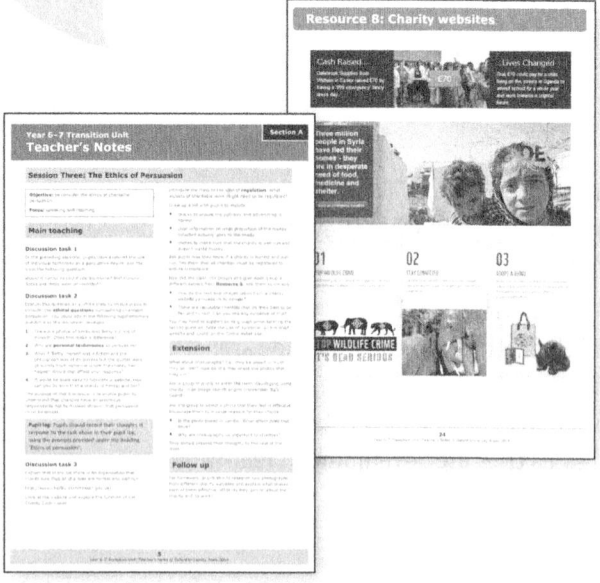

Transition support

Teacher Companion 1 includes English lesson suggestions and guidance on effective transition from Primary to Secondary school. It also includes a range of teaching ideas for the first week of English lessons in Secondary schools, with an opening lesson included in Student Book 1. In addition, there is a professional development unit specifically on transition in Kerboodle: Lessons, Resources and Assessment.

Also on Kerboodle LRA 1 and on the Oxford University Press *Ignite English* webpage, you will find a unit of work, with transition tips, for Primary school teachers to use in the final term of Year 6. This unit, 'Making a Difference', has *Ignite English* principles at its heart and we hope that by passing this unit on to local Primary schools it will foster enhanced relationships between Secondary school English departments and colleagues in local Primary schools.

Student Books

The Student Books have been designed to develop a range of reading, writing and spoken English skills in real life contexts. Each Student Book offers thematically-focused units, covering prose fiction, poetry, drama and non-fiction forms, as well as a focus on language and one unique immersive unit based around a real-world scenario. They also feature an explicit focus on spelling, punctuation and grammar (SPAG). There is a wide range of source texts and activities with Stretch and Support as well as regular Progress Checks and Extra Time features, which can be used either for extension or homework.

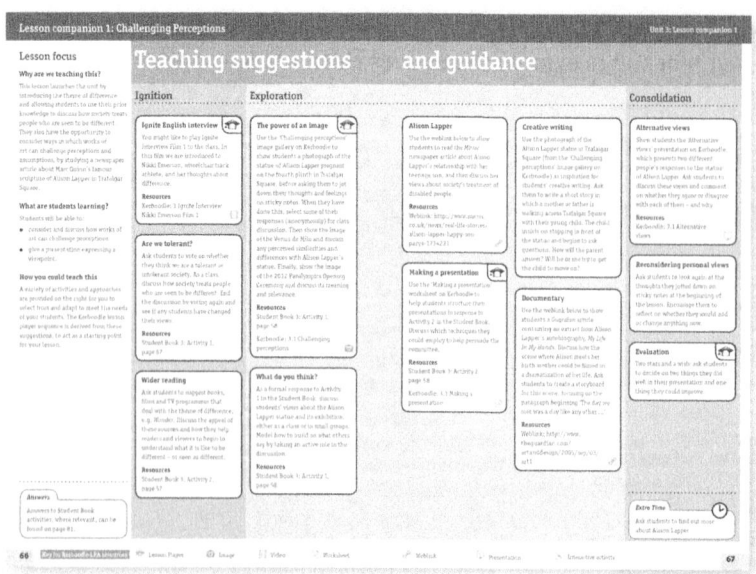

Teacher Companions

Each Teacher Companion shares the thinking and philosophy behind the resources with a focus on the 'why', 'what' and 'how' of each unit, lesson and assessment. Additionally, the Teacher Companions feature unit-by-unit teaching support materials with comprehensive teaching tips, links and further reading suggestions. Each lesson features a Lesson Companion that includes a range of teaching ideas, guidance and tips to enable you to customize your lessons. The Teacher Companion also includes guidance and suggestions on setting up and marking the end-of-unit assessments.

Kerboodle: Lessons, Resources and Assessment

Kerboodle is packed full of guided support and ideas for creating and running effective lessons. It's intuitive to use, customizable, and can be accessed online anytime and anywhere. *Ignite English* Kerboodle LRA includes:

- 18 exclusive interviews providing over 40 unique and compelling films, connecting the learning in KS3 English lessons to skills used in thematically-linked jobs

- Eight specially-commissioned filmed units providing CPD for English departments on key areas of Key Stage 3 teaching and learning, including genuine lesson footage, interviews with Primary and Secondary school teachers and students, and comments and observations from Geoff Barton and Phil Jarrett

- Materials to support the transition for students from Key Stage 2 to Key Stage 3

- Grammar support for teachers and students through extensive spelling, punctuation and grammar interactives and a grammar reference guide

- A wealth of additional resources including: interactive activities, an editable alternative end-of-unit assessment for every Student Book unit, marking scales to help monitor progress, photos, editable presentations, editable worksheets (general, differentiation and peer/self-assessment) and weblinks

- Lesson Player, enabling teachers to deliver ready-made lessons or the freedom to customize plans to suit your classes' needs

Sarah Pinborough, Horror writer: Horror is a feeling.

Kerboodle Online Student Books

All three student books are also available as Online Student Books. These can be accessed on a range of devices, such as tablets, and offer a bank of tools to enable students to personalize their book and view notes left by the teacher.

Ignite English Kerboodle: Lessons, Resources and Assessment is packed full of guided support and ideas for running and creating effective KS3 English lessons. It's intuitive to use, customizable, and can be accessed online. It also includes teacher access to the accompanying *Ignite English* Kerboodle Book.

Ignite English Kerboodle: Lessons, Resources and Assessment provides hundreds of lively built-in resources, including unique specially commissioned films, interactive activities, ready-to-go lesson presentations, and supported assessment tasks with marking guidance. You can adapt many of these resources to suit you and your students' individual needs and upload your existing resources so everything can be accessed from one location.

Lessons

Ready-to-play lesson presentations (Lesson Player) complement every lesson in the book. Each Lesson Player is easy to launch, and features a ready-made lesson derived from the Ignition, Exploration and Consolidation activities in the corresponding Lesson Companion found in the Teacher Companion. These ready-made lessons include: unit objectives, an Ignition activity, Exploration activities and a Consolidation activity plus all the relevant resources (such as **Ignite Interview** films, worksheets, images, interactive activities and presentations).

You can further personalize the lessons by adding in your own resources and notes or bringing in other resources from elsewhere in *Ignite English*. Your lessons and notes can be accessed by your whole department – they are a great time-saver and ideal for non-specialist teachers and cover lessons.

The Lessons module contains ready-to-play lesson plans and presentations that complement every lesson in the *Ignite English* Student Book

Resources are built into each Lesson Player so all the relevant activities, films and worksheets are ready to launch

For each lesson, a printable set of teacher notes are also available as a guide to support your lesson delivery, and provide further ideas or tips that only teachers can see

The resources you want to use can also be rearranged and launched in sequence to suit your classroom needs

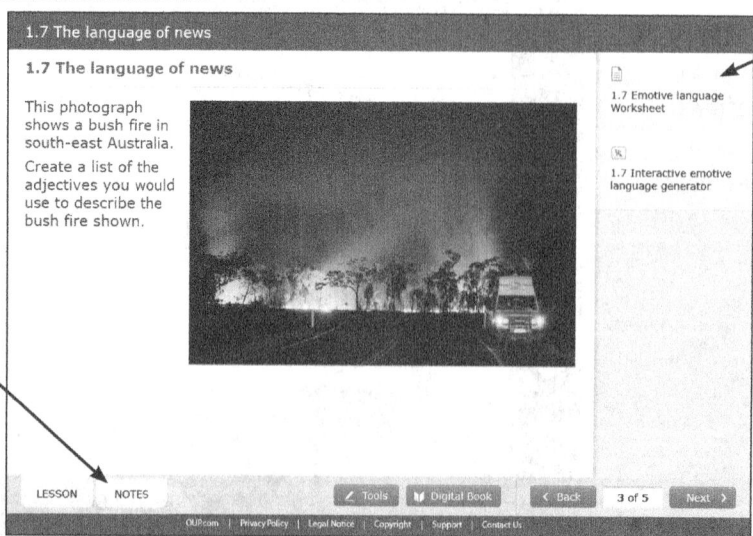

Ignite English Lesson Player

Resources

Ignite English Kerboodle: Lessons, Resources and Assessment has a wealth of resources for teachers and students. In **Kerboodle**, to access the full list of resources for *Ignite English*, click on the **Resources tab** at the top of the screen.

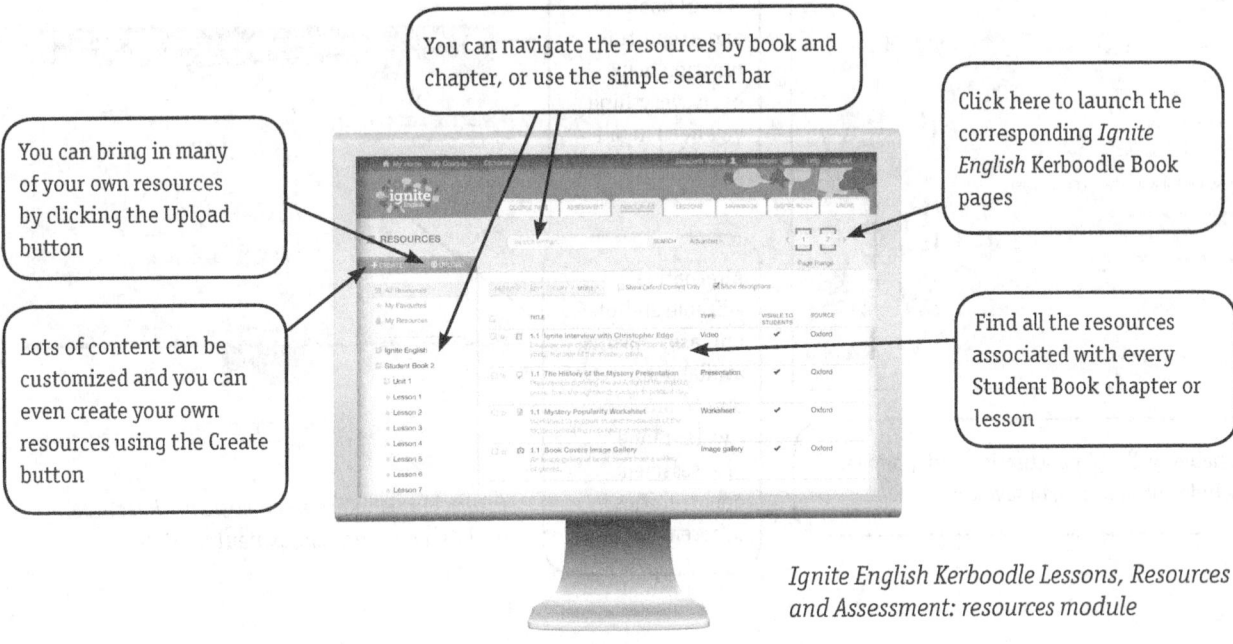

You can navigate the resources by book and chapter, or use the simple search bar

Click here to launch the corresponding *Ignite English* Kerboodle Book pages

You can bring in many of your own resources by clicking the Upload button

Lots of content can be customized and you can even create your own resources using the Create button

Find all the resources associated with every Student Book chapter or lesson

Ignite English Kerboodle Lessons, Resources and Assessment: resources module

Kerboodle resources are fully integrated with the *Ignite English* Student Books and Teacher Companions.

The resources module is packed full of Ignite Interview film clips, images, presentations, interactive activities and worksheets

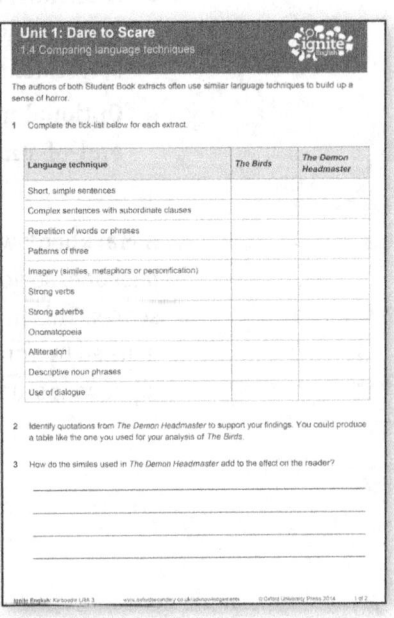

Worksheet on comparing language techniques from Kerboodle LRA 3, Unit 1: Dare to Scare

Assessment and Markbook

Click on the **Assessment tab** to find the assessment materials to help you deliver a varied and effective assessment programme.

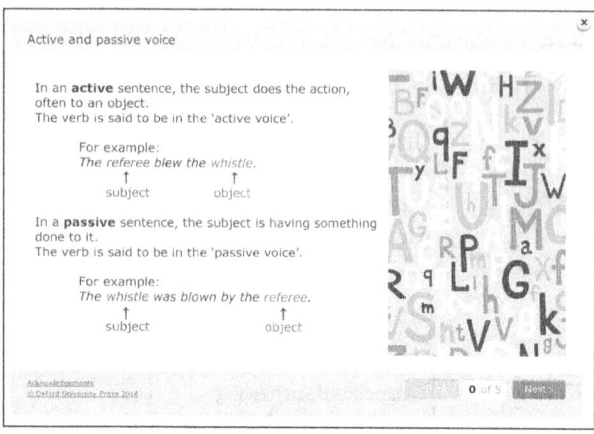

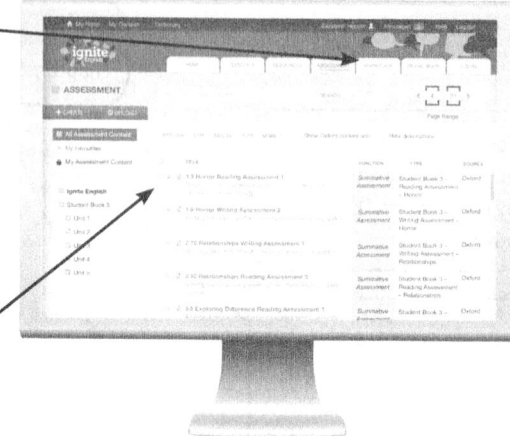

A markbook and a reporting function help keep everything you need in one place

Alternative editable end-of-unit assessments available for every unit to provide a wider range of assessment opportunities in different modes

A bank of assignable spelling, punctuation and grammar interactives include automarking to save time

Ignite English Kerboodle Lessons, Resources and Assessment: assessment module

The Assessment section provides:

- **SPAG interactives:** A bank of assignable spelling, punctuation and grammar interactive activities to help improve students' technical accuracy. Automarked interactives have marks automatically reported in the **Markbook**.

- **Alternative end-of-unit assessments:** Alternative editable end-of-unit assessments available for every Student Book unit to provide a wider range of assessment opportunities in different modes

- **Optional marking scales for use with reading, writing and spoken English end-of-unit assessments:** To help monitor progress

A **Markbook** with reporting functionality completes the Kerboodle assessment package, so you can keep track of all your students' test results and assessment scores. This includes both the auto-marked tests and work that needs to be marked by you. It is also easy to import class registers and create user accounts for all of your students.

Ignite English **Kerboodle Book**

Ignite English Kerboodle Book provides you with an on-screen version of the Student Book for use on your whiteboard with the whole class.

Teacher access to the *Ignite English* Kerboodle Book is **automatically available** as part of the Lessons, Resources and Assessment package. You can also choose to buy access for your students.

Both teacher and student access include a simple **bank of tools** so you can personalize the book and make notes.

It can be accessed on other devices, such as tablets.

You and your students can use different tools such as Sticky Notes, Bookmarks and Pencil features to personalize each page

You can Zoom in and Spotlight any part of the text

Every teacher and student has their own digital notebook for use within their Kerboodle Book

You can quickly navigate around the book with the contents menu or page number search

Unit overview

The chapters in this Teacher Companion link directly to the corresponding Student Book theme, but also aim to provide you with holistic thematic and practical support, both for planning and lesson delivery purposes. This starts with looking at the 'why', 'what' and 'how' for the unit as a whole, and then providing a snapshot medium-term outline. All of the subsequent ideas and guidance reflect the underpinning philosophy of *Ignite English*, allowing you the flexibility to adapt all the materials to suit the needs of your students, your department and your teaching style.

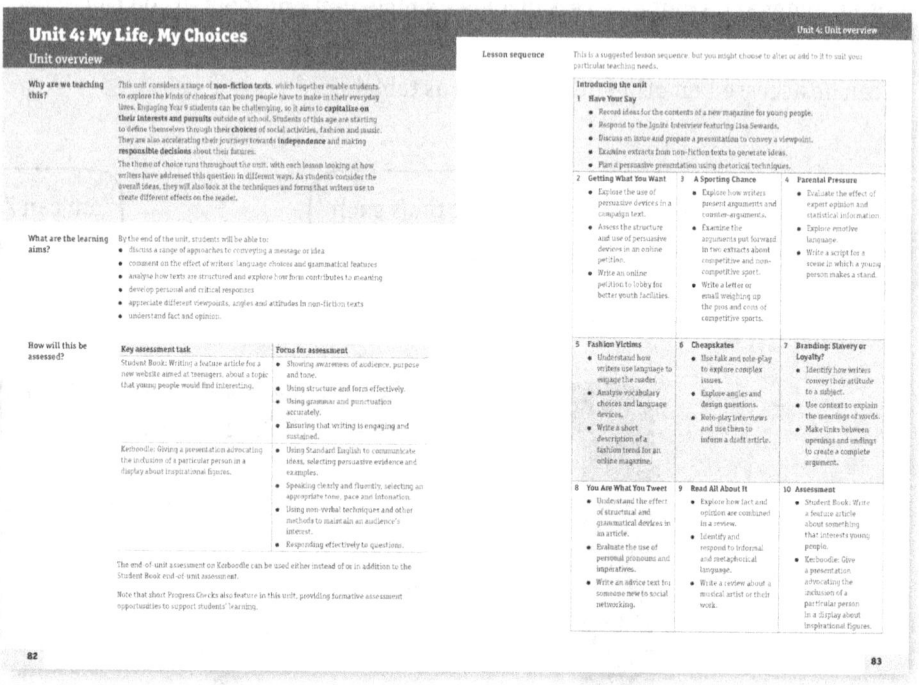

Preparing to teach

The preparing to teach sections in each chapter aim to equip you with useful background to the theme, saving you time but also enabling you to feel more confident when delivering the unit. Weblinks and wider reading, both for you and your students, is also included. Comprehensive practical teaching tips, in the context of the specific unit, conclude the preparing to teach section.

Lesson Companions

Each 'lesson' in the Student Book has a corresponding Lesson Companion in this Teacher Companion. The Lesson Companions open with sharing the 'why', 'what' and 'how' for each specific lesson. The main aim of each Lesson Companion is to provide you with a number of teaching ideas and tips, some of which relate to resources provided on the Kerboodle LRA, others are standalone. Guidance is also provided on Student Book activities. The intention is that from these lesson ideas you can create your own lessons, putting a selection of the ideas into a sequence or using some in parallel with different groups of students or individual students in your class. The Ignition, Exploration and Consolidation headings are a guide only – individual lesson ideas can be used in the way that suits your needs best. If you would like to follow a suggested route through the lesson ideas, these are indicated with the 🏠 symbol, and relate to the lesson sequence as it appears in the Kerboodle LRA Lesson Player.

The Lesson Companions also include guidance on the Extra Time Student Book features, which can be used either in class or as homework tasks. Additional Extra Time activities have been added to the Lesson Companions.

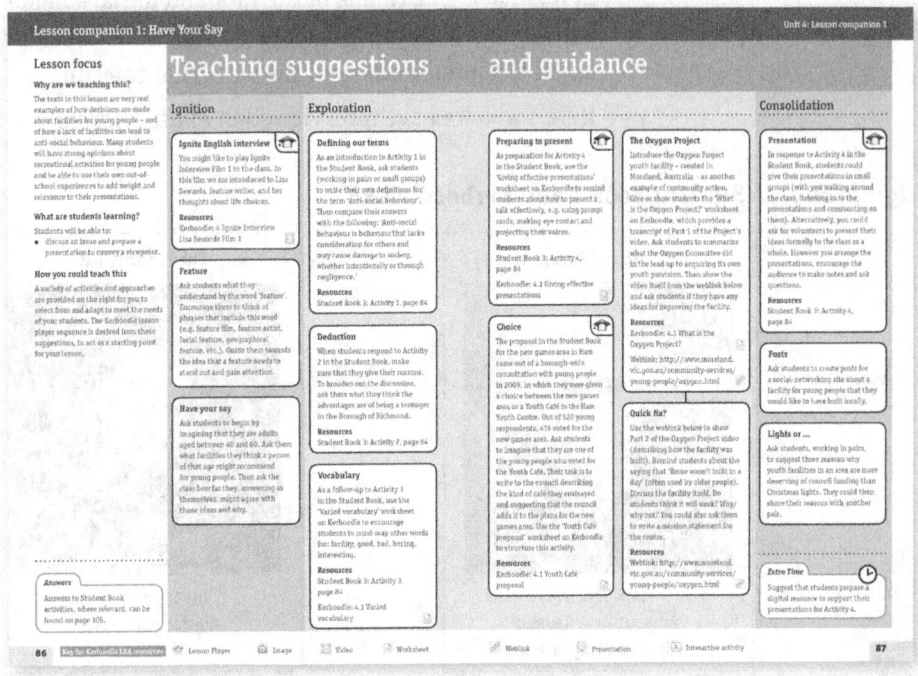

Assessment guidance and answers

Suggestions on how to set up and run the end-of-unit assessments is provided at the end of each chapter, together with guidance on marking. Answers to Student Book activities, where appropriate, are provided on the final page of each Teacher Companion chapter.

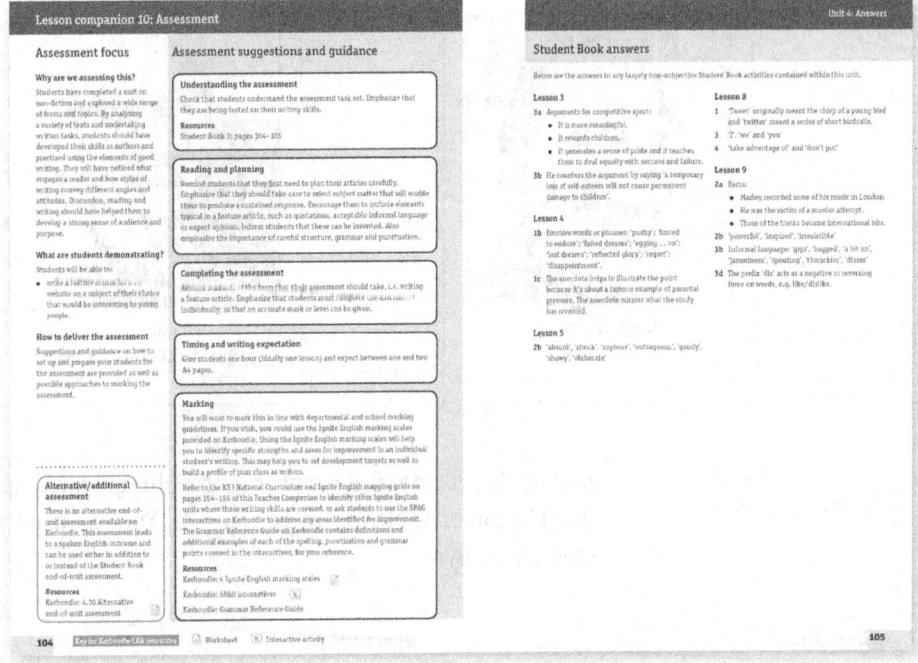

Ignite English features 18 specially-commissioned interviews, comprising over 40 films on Kerboodle: Lessons, Resources and Assessment. Introductions and quotations from the interviewees also appear throughout the Student Books.

These interviews, which are thematically linked to each Student Book unit, provide a direct connection for students with the relevant reading, writing or spoken English skills that they are developing in *Ignite English* and in English lessons generally.

The first film in every unit, and the introduction to every unit in the Student Books, provides an introduction to the interviewee, background to what they do in relation to the theme of the unit and initial comments on the skills they use. Subsequent films provide more specific skills comments and wider information about the interviewee and the work that they do.

Here's who we have interviewed in *Ignite English*:

Ignite English Student Book 1 and Kerboodle LRA 1

In Search of Adventure

Mick Conefrey,
Adventure writer and
documentary maker

The Identity Kit

Dreadlock Alien,
Performance poet

Out of This World

Jaine Fenn,
Science-fiction author

Travellers' Tales

Hugh Thomson,
Travel writer

Making the News

Will Gompertz,
BBC Arts Correspondent

Your Language

Maeve Diamond,
Accent and dialect coach

Kerboodle provides full support for teaching, learning and assessment but is also flexible and editable to suit your needs. You can use the lessons provided, or create your own.

Lessons
- Customizable lesson presentations and plans with resources launched directly from the presentation
- Teacher notes accompany every lesson
- Editable planning documents

Resources
- 18 specially-commissioned Ignite Interviews
- A wealth of photos, worksheets, presentations and interactive activities
- 8 specially-commissioned film-based CPD units
- Year 6 to Year 7 transition materials
- A comprehensive grammar guide

Assessment
- Alternative end-of-unit editable assessments
- A bank of assignable spelling, punctuation and grammar interactive activities
- Optional marking scales to help monitor progress
- Online markbook

Ignite English Student Book 2 and Kerboodle LRA 2

It's a Mystery

Christopher Edge,
Mystery writer

Words of War

Ed Boanas,
Infantry officer

Appearance and Reality

Debbie Korley,
Actress

Technology Matters

Tom Worsley,
Engineer

Campaign for a Cause

Kate Geary and Matthew Grainger,
Media and Communications at
Oxfam

Power of Communication

Dominic Gettins,
Advertising agency: Head of
writing

Ignite English Student Book 3 and Kerboodle LRA 3

Dare to Scare

Sarah Pinborough,
Horror writer

Relationships

Nick Cope,
Song-writer and musician

Exploring Difference

Nikki Emerson,
Wheelchair track athlete

My Life, My Choices

Lisa Sewards,
Feature writer

Young Entrepreneurs

Renée Watson,
Business owner

From Talking Drums to Tweets

Fiona McPherson,
Oxford English Dictionary editor

Unit 1: Dare to Scare

Unit overview

Why are we teaching this?

Horror has the power to move readers both emotionally and psychologically. This unit explores a variety of horror texts in order to address the question: 'How do horror stories scare us?' In doing so, the unit develops students' **close analysis of a writer's craft**, as well as **the comparison and evaluation of differing narrative approaches**. Students explore the genre by reading extracts from classic Gothic horror, modern horror fiction, a Tennyson poem, and Shakespeare's *Macbeth*. The unit also crosses genres into the futuristic terror of science fiction, with Patrick Ness, and explores the comedic touches deployed by Charlie Higson to both amuse and repulse a reader. This unit also provides a context for the exploration of **setting**, **characterization**, **atmosphere and themes**, as well as for studying **vocabulary and grammatical features**. This is a genre that many students choose to **read for pleasure**, so it can provide a motivating route into the study of Gothic classics, such as *Dracula*, by comparing them with modern masters of the genre, such as Susan Hill.

What are the learning aims?

By the end of the unit, students will be able to:

- analyse and respond to a range of differing viewpoints and themes in a variety of texts from the horror genre
- use literary and linguistic terminology precisely and support explanations with close textual references and quotations
- analyse in depth and detail literary and grammatical features, exploring their effects on readers, including connotation, imagery, irony and the impact of noun phrases
- establish and sustain distinctive character, point of view and voice in their own fiction writing – drawing on a wide range of techniques and devices used by writers.

How will this be assessed?

Key assessment task	Focus for assessment
Student Book: Reading and analysing three horror extracts and writing a reasoned report recommending one of them to be included in an anthology of horror writing for teenagers.	<ul><li>Analysing how writers depict setting, theme and characters.</li><li>Commenting on a range of literary techniques, e.g. vocabulary, imagery, and narrative voice.</li><li>Comparing and evaluating the effectiveness of horror extracts.</li></ul>
Kerboodle: Writing the opening for a horror story in two contrasting styles, with accompanying commentaries explaining language choices.	<ul><li>Creating an effective opening, drawing on a range of literary features to create atmosphere and tension.</li><li>Establishing an effective narrative voice, using a range of vocabulary, sentence structures and punctuation to create impact and drama.</li><li>Precise and confident use of literary and linguistic terminology in the accompanying commentaries.</li></ul>

The end-of-unit assessment on Kerboodle can be used either instead of or in addition to the Student Book end-of-unit assessment.

Note that short Progress Checks also feature in this unit, providing formative assessment opportunities to support the students' learning.

Lesson sequence

This is a suggested lesson sequence, but you might choose to alter or add to it to suit your particular teaching needs.

Introducing the unit

1 Sinister Settings

- Reactivate prior knowledge by discussing different frightening things and why people enjoy being scared by horror stories.
- Respond to the Ignite Interview with horror writer Sarah Pinborough.
- Analyse the themes and motifs of typical horror stories.
- Identify how a writer creates a feeling of fear.

---

2 From the Ordinary to the Extraordinary

- Analyse in detail how language can create atmosphere and build tension.
- Create noun phrases to convey a chilling mood.
- Compare their own noun phrases with those used by Elizabeth Bowen in an extract from *The Demon Lover*.

3 You're Welcome ...

- Use inference to explore characterization.
- Understand the use of irony.
- Read and analyse an extract from *Dracula*.
- Use inference and deduction to explore layers of meaning.

4 Attack!

- Comment on how writers use sentence structure, word choice and imagery to create impact and drama.
- Compare the techniques used to create horror in extracts from *The Birds* and *The Demon Headmaster*.
- Practise skills required for the end-of-unit assessment.

---

5 All in the Mind

- Explore a range of themes in psychological horror stories.
- Analyse themes and how they are presented in an extract from Tennyson's poem 'Tithonus'.

6 Graphic Detail

- Compare the effectiveness of graphic horror with psychological horror.
- Read an extract from *The Dead* and comment on Charlie Higson's use of language.
- Experiment with choosing vocabulary and imagery to write contrasting horror descriptions in both a graphic and a psychological style.

7 The Supernatural on Stage

- Experiment with different techniques of conveying horror in a dramatic scene.
- Compare and evaluate production photographs from Act 3, Scene 4 of *Macbeth*.
- Plan, present and evaluate a dramatized performance of the same scene.

---

8 Tenses and Tension

- Explore how verb tense influences the narrative voice and its effect on the reader.
- Investigate the effect of tenses and other language features on the creation of tension.
- Transform an extract from Patrick Ness' *The Knife of Never Letting Go* from one tense to another and compare its impact.

---

9 Assessment

- Student Book: Read, select and justify material for a horror anthology for teenagers.
- Kerboodle: Write the opening for a horror story in two contrasting styles.

Preparing to teach

Refresh your knowledge

You might find it helpful to refer to the following key points when planning your teaching of this unit.

- The roots of the horror genre can be traced back to the 18th century. The first Gothic horror novel is usually acknowledged to be Horace Walpole's *The Castle of Otranto* (1764), which established the conventions of the genre – a vulnerable romantic hero or heroine; an architecturally grand gothic setting; and sinister events which, at least on the surface, seem to have supernatural origins.

- During the Romantic period, the genre quickly evolved from sensationalized supernatural stories that were modelled on *The Castle of Otranto*. With rapid developments in science and medicine came a more pragmatic and realistic horror, such as Mary Shelley's *Frankenstein* (a book that enters the realms of science fiction). This subgenre of horror, which crosses into science fiction, continues to this day (with noteworthy examples including R. J. Materson's *I Am Legend* and the Chaos Walking series of teen novels written by Patrick Ness).

- In 19th-century America, Edgar Allan Poe adopted a psychological angle to his tales of terror – allowing readers an insight into his narrators' violent and disturbed psyches in short stories such as *The Tell-Tale Heart* (1843).

- Back in Britain, the onset of the 20th century (and the accompanying fin de siècle) inspired horror classics such as Robert Louis Stevenson's *The Strange Case of Dr Jekyll and Mr Hyde* (1886) and Oscar Wilde's *The Picture of Dorian Gray* (1890), both of which explored how debauched, depraved and immoral human beings could become in their quest for scientific advancement or immortality.

- The popularity of the horror genre flourished in the late 20th century, with Stephen King regularly topping bestseller lists on both sides of the Atlantic. Horror stories are also popular in children's fiction, with top-selling series including 'Point Horror' and 'Goosebumps'.

- Vampire fiction has also enjoyed something of a renaissance, with the teen phenomenon of Stephenie Meyer's hugely popular 'Twilight' series spawning a series of blockbusting films. It would seem that the desire be thrilled, shocked and unnerved is as great as ever.

Links and further reading

- As there are links to horror films within it, please use the following overview of the gothic fiction genre as a reference point for teachers only: http://www.gothic.net/category/fiction/

- The following website provides a forum for teens to share and read horror fiction: http://www.wattpad.com/stories/teen-fiction/horror

- The Horror Writers' Association website includes a link to texts nominated for Bram Stoker's Horror Award, as well as a list of recommended reads for young adults: http://www.horror.org/index.php

- The following website contains a list of recommended horror reads for teenagers to young adults, including useful overviews of the nature of the content (highlighting any which might cause distress or upset): http://www.monsterlibrarian.com/horrorfictionlistya.htm

- The Spinebreakers website is popular and well respected: http://www.spinebreakers.co.uk/books/list/?sort=genre&sort=genre&selected_genre=10. At the time of writing, there were only three books listed under the genre of horror, but you could recommend this site as a means of students posting reviews of books they read during this unit.

- Interactive activities, including games based on typical plots and scenarios featured in 'Goosebumps', can be found on the following website: http://www.scholastic.com/goosebumps/

- The website of Darren Shan, the popular writer of teen horror, includes extracts from his own works: http://www.darrenshan.com/

- Recommendations for students' independent reading: (Classic gothic horror) *Frankenstein* by Mary Shelley; *The Strange Case of Dr Jekyll and Mr Hyde* by Robert Louis Stevenson; *Wuthering Heights* by Emily Brontë; *Dracula* by Bram Stoker; (Contemporary teen horror) *My Swordhand is Singing* by Marcus Sedgewick; *A Greyhound of a Girl* by Roddy Doyle; *The Devil Walks* by Anne Fine; 'Enemy' series by Charlie Higson.

Please note that OUP is not responsible for third-party content. Although all links were correct at the time of publication, the content and location of this material may change.

Planning guidance and teaching tips

Think about how you can make the materials relevant to your students and responsive to their needs. Some suggested approaches to address key areas are provided below.

- Be mindful that, while many students will revel in the emotional and psychological thrills of this genre, others may find it disturbing. Give students the opportunity to express their concerns and offer them reassurance (providing less-disturbing texts for **sensitive students**).

- Whilst horror fiction can be a motivating genre for students, reading extracts from Victorian-era Gothic fiction can create challenges for **more-reluctant readers**, as well as **EAL** students. Be prepared to work with these students in one-to-one and guided group contexts to support their reading throughout the course of the unit. Consider strategies you could use to keep their interest and build their reading stamina (e.g. using quick **comprehension quizzes** to provide an element of competition to their reading).

- Students will use a range of reading strategies to help them engage with and respond to the texts in this unit, but a key focus for teaching and learning should be developing their skills of **inference** and **deduction** to explore layers of meaning. Ensure that students are aware of the distinction between inference and deduction, where deduction is to make a judgement about something based on information from the text, whilst inferences are opinions and hypotheses that draw on prior knowledge, personal engagement and clues from the text. Generally, inference requires more-complex reasoning on the part of the reader.

- Provide appropriate **differentiated** support for students' writing through the use of horror genre checklists, vocabulary banks, writing frames, dictionaries and thesauruses, etc. Ensure an appropriate level of challenge for **gifted and talented** students by encouraging more-confident writers to experiment with the conventions of the genre in their writing (e.g. by banning them from revealing the exact nature of the threat).

- Give students space to talk about and reflect on their reading. Creating opportunities for them to discuss and share ideas about a text can help to engage **more-reluctant readers** with negative attitudes towards reading.

- Refer to the **Grammar Reference Guide** on Kerboodle for definitions and exemplars of the specific grammatical features and literary devices covered in the unit.

- Aim to provide opportunities for students to work with real writers. The real context and purpose of the end-of-unit assessment task can help to motivate students' writing, but you could provide further inspiration and support by arranging for an author of horror stories to come into the classroom to share their perspective and advice as a writer.

- Encourage students to work in small groups and draw on their independent reading to produce a reading trail for the horror genre. This could be displayed in the school library to promote **reading for pleasure**. Give time in the classroom for students to discuss their independent reading.

Lesson focus

Why are we teaching this?

This lesson is designed to draw upon and reactivate students' prior knowledge of the genre by exploring horror motifs. As a foundation for later analysis, students consider the significance of these motifs and conduct a close reading of an extract from a classic horror story.

What are students learning?

Students will be able to:

- analyse the themes and motifs of typical horror stories.

How you could teach this

A variety of activities and approaches are provided on the right for you to select from and adapt to meet the needs of your students. The Kerboodle lesson player sequence is derived from these suggestions, to act as a starting point for your lesson.

Answers

Answers to Student Book activities, where relevant, can be found on page 37.

Teaching suggestions

Ignition

Ignite English interview

You might like to play Ignite Interview Film 1 to the class. In this film we are introduced to Sarah Pinborough, horror writer, and her thoughts about horror writing.

Resources

Kerboodle: 1 Ignite Interview Sarah Pinborough Film 1

Prior knowledge

Ask pairs of students to note down or draw typical settings for horror stories. Then ask them to discuss what makes these settings scary, before rank ordering them according to their potential to terrify a reader or viewer.

Sinister storytelling

Ask students to tell a terrifying tale, starting with 'It was a dark and stormy night …'. They could take it in turns to say a sentence each until they have created the scariest story they can. If possible, to create a more menacing atmosphere, students could tell their stories by torchlight in a darkened classroom.

Exploration

Motifs

To support differentiation, issue students with copies of the 'Horror motifs' worksheet on Kerboodle to support their work in response to Activity 1a in the Student Book.

Resources

Student Book 3: Activities 1a and 1b, page 10

Kerboodle: 1.1 Horror motifs

Name that genre game

Ask students to note down or draw motifs from a particular genre, such as romance or science fiction, before asking their partner to guess the genre. To provide stretch, students could explain the connotations of these motifs. This could be arranged as a sorting activity.

Colour connotations

Issue each student with two cards – one yellow and one blue. Ask them to write down the first season, emotion and natural object that come to mind when they think of each colour. Then ask them to share and compare their two lists with a partner. This could lead to a class discussion about the connotations of particular colours and how writers might use colour to evoke such connotations.

Key for Kerboodle LRA resources   Lesson Player   Image   Video    Worksheet

and guidance

Consolidation

Why red?

Ask students to discuss why H. G. Wells made the room red and what connotations he might have been trying to evoke by doing so.

Horror on film

Ask students to use the 'Storyboard template' worksheet on Kerboodle to storyboard the extract from *The Red Room* in the Student Book as a film to maximise the viewing audience's feelings of terror. Ask them to consider sound effects as well as the images that would appear on screen.

Resources
Kerboodle: 1.1 Storyboard template

Horror context

Use the 'History of Horror' presentation on Kerboodle to discuss the literary and historical context of the horror genre. Draw students' attention to the impacts of scientific and cultural developments in society on the genre.

Resources
Kerboodle: 1.1 History of Horror

Understanding *The Red Room*

To accompany Activities 2 and 3 in the Student Book, use the 'True-or-false quiz' interactive activity on Kerboodle to support differentiation and check students' understanding of the extract.

Resources
Student Book 3: Activities 2 and 3, page 11

Kerboodle: 1.1 True-or-false quiz

A sinister setting

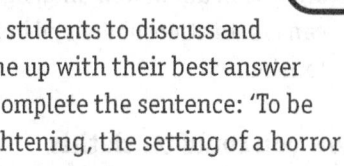

Ask students to describe a sinister setting of their own, by deploying some of the horror motifs and techniques used in the extract from *The Red Room*.

Debating the narrator's actions

Set up a debate about whether the narrator is brave or insane to enter the Red Room, knowing that the previous person who dared to do so met a mysterious end. Support differentiation by assigning statements to argue for or against, e.g. 'He's brave, because he knows that he could be in danger'; 'He's insane, because he's putting his life at risk'.

Enhancing fear

Write the nouns used in the Student Book extract from *The Red Room* onto cards and place them around the classroom. Then ask students to stand next to the one that they believe most contributes to the feeling of fear in the extract. Ask for volunteers to explain their choices.

Summarizing scariness

Ask students to discuss and come up with their best answer to complete the sentence: 'To be frightening, the setting of a horror story must …'

Terror tennis

Ask students to call out horror motifs (nouns), while their partner has five seconds to respond with an appropriately menacing adjective. For example, *moonlight – ghostly*. To add challenge, you could insist that the adjective is alliterative.

Extra Time

Ask students to write the next few paragraphs of *The Red Room*, continuing on from the end of the Student Book extract in the same style.

Lesson focus

Why are we teaching this?

This lesson is designed to foster students' creativity by giving them the opportunity to experiment with language and its effects. Pivotal to this is an especially evocative and atmospheric description of a sinister setting from a short story called *The Demon Lover* by Elizabeth Bowen. To develop their skills as critical readers, students have to compare noun phrases which they have created with those that Elizabeth Bowen uses to make an everyday setting take on a menacing mood.

What are students learning?

Students will be able to:

- analyse in detail how language can create atmosphere and build tension.

How you could teach this

A variety of activities and approaches are provided on the right for you to select from and adapt to meet the needs of your students. The Kerboodle lesson player sequence is derived from these suggestions, to act as a starting point for your lesson.

Teaching suggestions

Ignition

Spooky speculation

Show students the nouns and adjectives displayed in Activity 1. Ask them to note down whom or what they might be describing before sharing and discussing their ideas with a partner.

Resources
Student Book 3: Activity 1, page 12

Revising word classes

Show students a list of words from *The Demon Lover* extract and ask them to identify the nouns and the adjectives. This could be achieved actively, by giving each student a card featuring one of these words and asking them to stand in an area of the room to signify whether the word is a noun or an adjective.

Noun phrases generator

Continuing the active approach of the idea above, ask students to stand next to a partner to form an effective noun phrase and discuss why it's effective before sharing their explanation with the rest of the group.

Exploration

Contextualizing horror

Show 'The Blitz' image gallery on Kerboodle and ask students to discuss when and where these images might have been taken. They should then discuss why this would make an apt setting for a ghost story, before identifying other examples of writers playing upon the fears of society at a time they were writing about.

Resources
Kerboodle: 1.2 The Blitz

Sharing sinister settings

Follow up Activity 1b in the Student Book by asking student volunteers to read out their best noun phrases. Then ask the rest of the class to rate them for scariness (perhaps using score cards).

Resources
Student Book 3: Activities 1a and 1b, page 12

Silly settings

Ask students to experiment with antonyms and transform their sinister noun phrases from Activity 1b in the Student Book into silly ones.

Answers

Answers to Student Book activities, where relevant, can be found on page 37.

and guidance

Textual analysis

Use the 'Textual analysis' worksheet on Kerboodle to support students' analysis of the extract from *The Demon Lover* on page 13 of the Student Book.

Resources

Student Book 3: Activities 2 and 3, page 13

Kerboodle: 1.2 Textual analysis

Terror radio

Ask students, working in pairs or small groups, to produce a radio-friendly performance of *The Demon Lover* extract in the Student Book. Allow them to include appropriate sound effects to help build the tension and terror.

What happens next?

Following on from the extract in the Student book, ask students to discuss and predict what might happen next in *The Demon Lover*. You could even ask them to write a continuation of the story.

Ignite English interview

You might like to play Ignite Interview Film 1 to the class. In this film we are introduced to Sarah Pinborough and her thoughts about horror writing.

Resources

Kerboodle: 1 Ignite Interview Sarah Pinborough Film 1

A ghastly ghostly ending

Ask students to read, or read to them, the rest of *The Demon Lover* short story.

The Others

Show students the scene from the film *The Others* when Nicole Kidman's character enters a room where furniture is covered in sheets (this occurs 32 minutes into the film and lasts for about 2 minutes). Ask students to compare this with the extract from *The Demon Lover* in the Student Book.

Extra Time

Ask students to read again H. G. Wells' description of a sinister setting on page 11 of the Student Book. Then ask them to respond in writing to the question: 'What similarities are there between Bowen's description of her setting and that of *The Red Room* by H. G. Wells?' Ask students to explain which description they find the most frightening and why.

Consolidation

Progress Check

To check their understanding of the conventions of the horror genre, ask students to use the 'Progress Check' worksheet on Kerboodle to write a description that turns an everyday scene into a sinister and threatening one – worthy of a horror story.

Resources

Kerboodle: 1.2 Progress Check

Updating the horror

Ask students to come up with a modern everyday setting that could be used to create a similarly unsettling mood to that in *The Demon Lover*.

Summarizing sinister settings

Ask students, working individually, to sum up the three main things required to make a setting sinister. Then ask them to move into small groups and discuss their thoughts in order to reach a consensus.

 Weblink   🖥 Presentation   🔖 Interactive activity

Lesson focus

Why are we teaching this?

This lesson focuses on another key feature of the horror genre – characterization. It introduces students to an iconic and archetypical Gothic villain, Bram Stoker's Count Dracula. To develop their skills as critical readers further, students use inference and close textual analysis, including that of irony, and support their points with textual evidence.

What are students learning?

Students will be able to:
- use inference to explore characterization
- understand the use of irony.

How you could teach this

A variety of activities and approaches are provided on the right for you to select from and adapt to meet the needs of your students. The Kerboodle lesson player sequence is derived from these suggestions, to act as a starting point for your lesson.

> **Answers**
>
> Answers to Student Book activities, where relevant, can be found on page 37.

Teaching suggestions

Ignition

Movie vampires

Show students the 'Movie vampires' image gallery on Kerboodle, which displays a series of images of actors from different movie periods all portraying vampires. Ask students to discuss, in pairs or small groups, how they would sequence these images from the oldest to the most recent portrayal. Then ask them to discuss how and why they think the way vampires have been portrayed has changed over time. Finally, ask them to explain which of the dramatic portrayals they find the most frightening and why.

Resources
Kerboodle: 1.3 Movie vampires 📷

Fear on film

Ask students to imagine that they have one minute to pitch an idea to a top Hollywood film producer for a new horror film called *Fear*. Working in pairs, each partner should pitch their idea and then discuss which is the most effective and why. Also ask them to discuss how their ideas compare with those features they might find in any horror book or film.

Terrifying top trumps

Ask students to list three categories they would use to rate how frightening a character in a horror story might be, e.g. appearance. Have them discuss and agree their choices with a partner. They could revisit these categories later and rate Dracula, as he is described in the Student Book extract, against them.

Exploration

Visualizing a vampire

Ask students to sketch a typical vampire. Then read the extract from *Dracula* on page 14 of the Student Book and ask them to discuss how and why their drawing is similar to or different from the description of Count Dracula in the extract.

Researching origins

Ask students to conduct some research into the origins of the vampire myth and the inspiration behind Dracula – the historical figure Vlad the Impaler. Ask why Bram Stoker might have created the character of Count Dracula at this point in history. *Warning:* this activity could get gory, so it's not for the faint-hearted student.

Analysing character

To support differentiation, offer students the 'Scaffolding analysis' worksheet on Kerboodle to support their overall analysis of the extract on page 14 of the Student Book.

Resources
Student Book 3: Activities 1–3, page 15

Kerboodle: 1.3 Scaffolding analysis

and guidance

Consolidation

'Courtly' analysis

You could follow up Activity 1b in the Student Book and stretch students by asking them to research the origins of the word 'courtly'. They should then explain what this knowledge adds to their impression of the Count's behaviour.

Resources
Student Book 3: Activity 1b, page 15

Vampires on film

Show students age-appropriate clips of vampires on film. Possible choices include Bela Lugosi's 1931 film *Dracula* and *Nosferatu* from 1922. Ask them to analyse what these clips reveal about the cinematic techniques used to create a mood of fear. Ask individual students which clip is the most frightening and why, or take a class vote.

Dramatizing Dracula

Ask students to work in pairs to dramatize the meeting between Jonathan Harker and Count Dracula. Say that they should use a range of dramatic techniques to emphasize Dracula's strange and unsettling behaviour and explore Harker's reactions.

Dracula continues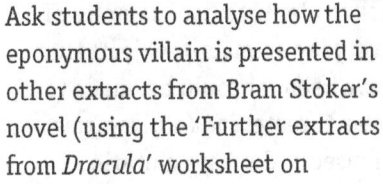

Ask students to analyse how the eponymous villain is presented in other extracts from Bram Stoker's novel (using the 'Further extracts from *Dracula*' worksheet on Kerboodle).

Resources
Kerboodle: 1.3 Further extracts from *Dracula*

22nd-century vampires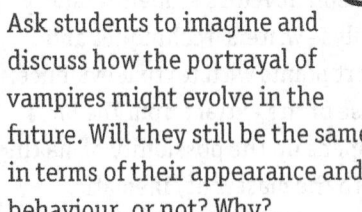

Ask students to imagine and discuss how the portrayal of vampires might evolve in the future. Will they still be the same in terms of their appearance and behaviour, or not? Why?

More menace

Ask students to write a description implying that a character is hiding a dark secret.

Hierarchy of horror

Ask students to rank-order iconic monsters, according to how frightening they find them and why (e.g. Frankenstein, werewolves and mummies).

Extra Time

Ask students to continue writing their horror stories. Encourage them to read their stories through and edit them to make them more effective.

 Weblink   Presentation   Interactive activity

Lesson focus

Why are we teaching this?

This lesson focuses upon another key element of the horror genre – how writers create impact and drama through sentence structure, word choice and imagery. By doing so, the lesson develops students' ability to analyse writers' techniques and support points with textual evidence. The use of the extract from *The Birds* also opens up the possibility of making links to the master of cinematic suspense, Alfred Hitchcock, through analysis of posters and stills from the film. Comparing two extracts in which innocent victims are under attack also enables students to practise and consolidate their skills of textual analysis and evaluation prior to completing the end-of-unit assessment.

What are students learning?

Students will be able to:

- comment on how writers use sentence structure, word choice and imagery to create impact and drama.

How you could teach this

A variety of activities and approaches are provided on the right for you to select from and adapt to meet the needs of your students. The Kerboodle lesson player sequence is derived from these suggestions, to act as a starting point for your lesson.

Answers

Answers to Student Book activities, where relevant, can be found on page 37.

Teaching suggestions

Ignition

Everyday horror

Ask students to list examples of everyday animals or objects that have been, or could be, made to seem threatening (e.g. swarms of insects, diseases mutating). Discuss why writers might choose to ground their horror stories in the everyday, rather than in supernatural or otherworldly phenomena. Ask students to discuss whether they think the everyday or the otherworldly has the potential to be the most frightening.

Prediction of peril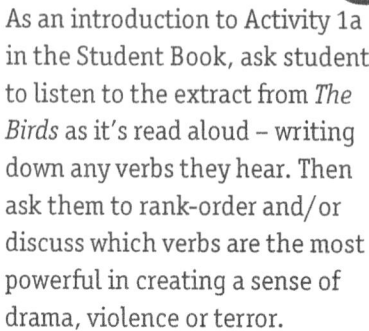

Write the opening sentence from *The Birds* extract on page 16 of the Student Book on the board: 'Covering his head with his arms he ran towards the cottage.' Ask students to discuss and predict what might be causing the threat or danger here. Explain that this quotation comes from a horror story called *The Birds*, and ask students to discuss whether or not they find this surprising and why.

Flights of fancy

Before they read Daphne du Maurier's description on page 16 of the Student Book, ask students to describe a bird attack in as menacing and threatening a way as possible.

Exploration

The value of verbs

As an introduction to Activity 1a in the Student Book, ask students to listen to the extract from *The Birds* as it's read aloud – writing down any verbs they hear. Then ask them to rank-order and/or discuss which verbs are the most powerful in creating a sense of drama, violence or terror.

Resources

Student Book 3: Activity 1a, page 16

Analysing Nat's terror

To support differentiation in Activity 2, provide some students with the quotations on the 'Analysing Nat's terror' worksheet, so that they can match them with the language features listed in the grid.

Resources

Student Book 3: Activity 2, page 17

Kerboodle: 1.4 Analysing Nat's terror

and guidance

Consolidation

Still scary

Ask students to analyse how the still from Hitchcock's version of *The Birds* (provided on Kerboodle) creates a sense of fear and tension. Focus them on how the birds are made to seem threatening, as well as the reaction of the actors. Support differentiation by modelling a mind-map to answer the question.

Resources
Kerboodle: 1.4 A still from Hitchcock's *The Birds*

A still scary story

Ask students to write a description based on the film still from *The Birds*, using the range of techniques used by Daphne du Maurier to create horror.

Storyboard

Ask students to storyboard the extract from *The Birds* in the Student Book – as it might appear in a film.

Resources
Kerboodle: 1.4 Storyboard template

Petrifying posters

Following up Activity 3 in the Student Book, use the 'Petrifying posters' image gallery on Kerboodle to show students a selection of posters from classic horror films. Ask them to compare how these posters create a mood of fear, e.g. through colour, imagery, motifs, etc.

Resources
Student Book 3: Activity 3, page 17

Kerboodle: 1.4 Petrifying posters

Horrific Head Teacher

Ask students to describe their own Head Teacher to make him or her seem as threatening and sinister as possible. Ask them to discuss why a Head Teacher makes an apt villain for a children's horror story.

Scaffolding the comparison

To support differentiation in Activities 4a and 4b in the Student Book, you could use the 'Comparing language techniques' worksheet on Kerboodle to provide students with further guidance and support.

Resources
Student Book 3: Activities 4a and 4b, page 19

Kerboodle: 1.4 Comparing language techniques

Tracking progress

Ask students to rank-order or R.A.G. rate the skills they have developed in this unit so far, using the bullet points in Activity 4b, according to how confident they are with each one.

A–Z

Ask students to create an A–Z of horror, based on their learning so far in this unit. A competitive element could be introduced by running this as a team competition against the clock.

Progress Check

Ask students to look at their partner's ratings and help them set a target for future improvement. For example, 'In order to make progress, I must …'.

Resources
Student Book 3: Progress Check, page 19

Extra Time

Ask students to write a description of an attack by an everyday object, or usually normal person – using techniques from the two extracts featured in this lesson. They could also write a commentary on their own writing, explaining the techniques they have used to create drama and tension.

 Weblink   Presentation   Interactive activity

Lesson focus

Why are we teaching this?

This lesson requires students to move beyond the analysis of individual extracts and towards an appreciation of common horror themes. In particular, it addresses recurring themes central to psychological horror stories (as the basis for later textual analysis and for possible inclusion in students' own compositions). The text studied in this lesson, Tennyson's poem 'Tithonus', also encourages progress in terms of the complexity of theme and vocabulary.

What are students learning?

Students will be able to:
- explore a range of themes in psychological horror stories.

How you could teach this

A variety of activities and approaches are provided on the right for you to select from and adapt to meet the needs of your students. The Kerboodle lesson player sequence is derived from these suggestions, to act as a starting point for your lesson.

Answers

Answers to Student Book activities, where relevant, can be found on page 37.

Teaching suggestions

Ignition

Types of terror

Ask students to discuss the different types of horror featured in books and films. Lead the discussion towards identifying two main types of horror – graphic and psychological – and discuss the differences between the two. Ask students to vote on which type of horror they find the most frightening. Using the 'Most scary' interactive activity on Kerboodle, discuss the different scenarios and ask students to rank them in order of horror.

Resources
Kerboodle: 1.5 Most scary

Movie horror

Reuse the 'Petrifying posters' image gallery on Kerboodle for this activity (Lesson 4). Show students the horror film posters and ask them to sort them into two groups, according to whether they adopt a graphic or a more psychological approach to horror. Discuss their differences and ask which ones students find the most frightening and why.

Resources
Kerboodle: 1.4 Petrifying posters

Terror topics

Ask students to list common fears within our society. They could then work with a partner or small group to discuss which ones are modern and which ones keep reoccurring through the generations.

Exploration

Human fears

To support differentiation in Student Book Activity 1, use the 'Human fears' presentation on Kerboodle to give students further statements about human fears.

Resources
Student Book 3: Activity 1, page 20

Kerboodle: 1.5 Human fears

Playing on fears

Ask students to list examples of books or films that play upon the fears identified in Activity 1.

Resources
Student Book 3: Activity 1, page 20

Walk of fear

As a prelude to Activity 2 in the Student Book, display signs around the room that name the main horror themes (e.g. death, disease). Ask students to move to the theme they find most frightening. Then ask for several volunteers to explain their choices.

Resources
Student Book 3: Activity 2, page 20

and guidance

Consolidation

Tithonus' terror

To support differentiation in Student Book Activities 4a–4c, provide students who require it with the 'Tithonus' terror' worksheet on Kerboodle to support their analysis of the poem.

Resources

Student Book 3: Activities 4a–4c, page 21

Kerboodle: 1.5 Tithonus' terror

Mythological menace

Ask students to research the etymology of the word 'phobia' and its relationship to the myth of the Greek god of fear, Phobos.

Imagining immortality

Ask students to debate the benefits and disadvantages of immortality. Support differentiation by providing students with prompting statements, such as: 'It would be great to live forever, because …' and 'It would be awful to outlive all our friends and family'.

The whole poetic picture

To support differentiation and provide stretch, you could share the whole of the poem 'Tithonus' with students, using the weblink below. Ask them what else they learn about Tithonus and the poem's moral message from the complete poem.

Resources

Weblink: http://www.poemhunter.com/poem/tithonus/

Ranking fears

Ask students to rank-order the psychological fears they have analysed in this lesson – according to how frightening they find them and how common they are in horror stories. Ask them to give reasons for their answers.

Psychological checkpoint

Ask students to finish this sentence: 'The type of horror I find most frightening is graphic/psychological (choose one) because …'

Tithonus today

Ask students to rewrite the Tithonus myth as a modern story – perhaps relating the quest for immortality to the current obsession with staying young.

Extra Time

The poem 'Tithonus' is based on the ancient Greek myth about Tithonus and Eos. Ask students to find out more about this story and be prepared to explain it in full.

 Weblink   🖥 Presentation   🔲 Interactive activity

Lesson focus

Why are we teaching this?

This lesson is designed to introduce students to a more graphic approach towards creating horror. They will explore a graphic zombie horror extract and evaluate its impact compared to horror writing, which favours a psychological approach. By doing so, students will develop skills of close textual analysis and demonstrate their understanding of contrasting styles of horror writing in preparation for the end-of-unit assessment.

What are students learning?

Students will be able to:

● compare the effectiveness of graphic horror with psychological horror.

How you could teach this

A variety of activities and approaches are provided on the right for you to select from and adapt to meet the needs of your students. The Kerboodle lesson player sequence is derived from these suggestions, to act as a starting point for your lesson.

Teaching suggestions

Ignition

Early graphic horror

Ask students to explore early examples of graphic horror, such as the description of Carew's death in *The Strange Case of Dr Jekyll and Mr Hyde* by Robert Louis Stevenson (supplied on Kerboodle). Ask them how they think a Victorian reader might have reacted to this, and whether many modern readers would react differently. Also ask them to give reasons for their responses.

Resources
Kerboodle: 1.6 Early graphic horror extract

Defining horror

Recap on the work from the previous lesson by asking students to write definitions of 'psychological horror' and 'graphic horror'.

Psychological versus graphic horror

Ask students to discuss the horror stories they have encountered. Do they prefer psychological or graphic horror? Which do they find more frightening and why?

Exploration

The graphic versus the ridiculous

Use the 'Graphic or ridiculous?' worksheet on Kerboodle to support differentiation in Student Book Activities 1a and 1b, by providing students with a list of quotations from the extract on page 22 to sort into those that are either 'grossly graphic' or 'repulsively ridiculous'. Then ask them to explain the effect of each quotation and rank-order them according to how frightening or funny they are.

Resources
Student Book 3: Activities 1a–1c, page 22

Kerboodle: 1.6 Graphic or ridiculous?

Exploring psychological horror

Support Activity 1d in the Student Book by issuing students with copies of the 'Exploring psychological horror' worksheet on Kerboodle. Ask them to compare its psychological horror style with the graphic extract on page 22 of the Student Book.

Resources
Student Book 3: Activity 1d, page 22

Kerboodle: 1.6 Exploring psychological horror

Answers
Answers to Student Book activities, where relevant, can be found on page 37.

and guidance

Consolidation

'We are all, in the end, just meat'

Ask students to debate Charlie Higson's statement at the end of the interview extract on page 23 of the Student Book. To support differentiation, some students could be provided with statements to argue for or against, such as: 'It's good to remember that we are all just meat, because it stops us from becoming too vain.' and 'Humans are far more than just meat – we are unique and intelligent individuals.'

Authorial viewpoint

Use the 'Authorial quotations' presentation on Kerboodle to share other quotations from different horror writers. Ask students to discuss whether they agree or disagree with each one.

Resources
Kerboodle: 1.6 Authorial quotations

Ignite English interview

You might like to play Ignite Interview Film 1 to the class. In this film we are introduced to Sarah Pinborough and her thoughts about horror writing.

Resources
Kerboodle: 1 Ignite Interview Sarah Pinborough Film 1

Zombie origins?

Provide students with a description of Frankenstein's monster, by issuing them with copies of the 'Frankenstein's monster' worksheet on Kerboodle. Then ask them to compare it with how the zombie teachers are presented in the extract from *The Dead* in the Student Book. Ask them to think about how Shelley makes Frankenstein a figure worthy of fear and pity, rather than of ridicule.

Resources
Kerboodle: 1.6 Frankenstein's monster

Monster images

Show the 'Monster mash' image gallery on Kerboodle to provide students with ideas about which monster to describe in both a graphic and a psychological way.

Resources
Student Book 3: Activities 2a–2c, page 23

Kerboodle: 1.6 Monster mash

Horror vote

Ask students to vote on which type of horror they find the most frightening – psychological or graphic. Then ask volunteers to explain the reasons for their choices.

The desensitization of the masses

Hold a class debate on the subject of whether students think graphic horror on TV and in films is causing our society to become more violent.

Progress Check

Ask students to use a Venn diagram to compare the features of graphic and psychological horror, supporting their points with examples from their own descriptions in response to Activities 2a and 2b.

Extra Time

Ask students to read the first of Charlie Higson's futuristic 'Enemy' series of novels, called *The Enemy*, which is about a disease that turns adults into zombies.

Lesson focus

Why are we teaching this?

This lesson broadens the range of literary genres which students study in this unit by asking them to consider and apply a variety of dramatic techniques used to build tension and terror. Focusing on a scene from *Macbeth* also offers the opportunity to study a text from a different historical and social context to those previously studied during the unit.

What are students learning?

Students will be able to:

- experiment with different techniques of conveying horror in a dramatic scene.

How you could teach this

A variety of activities and approaches are provided on the right for you to select from and adapt to meet the needs of your students. The Kerboodle lesson player sequence is derived from these suggestions, to act as a starting point for your lesson.

Teaching suggestions

Ignition

Ghostly goings on

Review students' prior knowledge by asking them to list as many ghost stories as they can.

Historical context

Ask students, working in pairs or small groups, to discuss why people in Shakespeare's time might have feared the supernatural more than we tend to do today. If they need some assistance to get them started, ask them to consider the impact of religious belief in the 16th century, as well as their more-limited scientific understanding of the world.

Ghastly ghosts

Ask students to discuss the following questions: 'Why are ghosts an enduring feature of the horror genre?'; 'What makes them frightening?'; 'Which of our fears do they play upon?'

Exploration

Comparing dramatizations

Support Activities 1a and 1b in the Student Book by giving students further images/stills of productions of the banquet scene, or show them different video versions (searching online for 'Macbeth banquet scene' will bring up lots of different options). Ask students to sort or sequence the various examples, based on different criteria. For example: how frightening they are; whether the ghost is presented in physical form; the reaction of the guests.

Resources
Student Book 3: Activities 1a and 1b, page 24

Dramatizing the scene

To support differentiation for Activity 2 in the Student Book, issue those students who need it with the 'Preparing to dramatize the scene' worksheet on Kerboodle.

Resources
Student Book 3: Activity 2, page 24

Kerboodle: 1.7 Preparing to dramatize the scene

Answers

Answers to Student Book activities, where relevant, can be found on page 37.

and guidance

Consolidation

Tableau of terror

Ask the groups to create a tableau, or freeze-frame, of the moment in their dramatization when they feel the audience will be most terrified. You could photograph these, before printing or uploading them in a format that students can annotate to explain how terror is created.

Ghostly monologue

To stretch students, ask them to imagine that the ghost of Banquo is given a monologue in which he speaks his thoughts and feelings aloud to an audience. You could ask them to write or perform what the ghost might say.

Transforming text

Ask students to adapt a prose extract from this unit to create a scene from a play (for later performance), with the aim of terrifying their audience.

Macbeth and Lady Macbeth

Ask students to make notes about what they learn about the personalities of the Macbeths in the banquet scene. How far do their characters support or challenge gender stereotypes?

Macbeth on film

Following their own performances and evaluation, show students clips of the banquet scene from previous productions (searching online for 'Macbeth banquet scene' will bring up lots of different options). Ask them to evaluate the clips using the same criteria they used to rate their own dramatizations.

Extra Time

Ask students to re-imagine the banquet scene from *Macbeth* in a more-modern setting, and to be prepared to explain their decisions. Ask them to consider carefully where and when they would set the action in order to maintain the psychological horror – and also to convey the Macbeths' high social status.

Summarizing dramatic techniques

Ask the different groups to list the techniques they used to make their performances tense and dramatic, e.g. intentional pauses, tone of voice. Then ask them to rank the techniques according to which were the most effective at creating a tense and dramatic mood for the audience.

Stage or page?

Ask students to discuss whether reading a text alone, or watching a performance with others, is a more-frightening experience. Ask them to give reasons for their answers.

Progress Check

Ask students to use the 'Performance Progress Check' worksheet on Kerboodle to write a review of another group's performance – describing and rating the effectiveness of the dramatic techniques used.

Resources

Kerboodle: 1.7 Performance Progress Check

Lesson focus

Why are we teaching this?

To build grammatical awareness and understanding, students revise the present and past tenses and analyse how the tense of a text can affect how dramatic it is. They consciously consider the impact of narrative perspective and tense on reader reaction, before writing an imagined continuation of the extract to develop their own ability to control perspective and tense.

What are students learning?

Students will be able to:

● explore how verb tense influences the narrative voice and its effect on the reader.

How you could teach this

A variety of activities and approaches are provided on the right for you to select from and adapt to meet the needs of your students. The Kerboodle lesson player sequence is derived from these suggestions, to act as a starting point for your lesson.

Answers

Answers to Student Book activities, where relevant, can be found on page 37.

Teaching suggestions

Ignition

The past versus the present tense

Issue copies of the 'Muddled tenses' worksheet on Kerboodle and ask students to revise the difference between the tenses by eliminating the inconsistencies in the passage. Use the 'Past and present tenses' interactive activity on Kerboodle to test students' understanding.

Resources

Kerboodle: 1.8 Muddled tenses

Kerboodle: 1.8 Past and present tenses

Future horrors

Ask students to identify the crossover between horror and science fiction by listing futuristic fears played upon in science-fiction stories, e.g. plague, environmental disaster.

Dystopian horror

Show students stills from dystopian science-fiction horror films, such as *The Day After Tomorrow*. Ask them to identify the genre of the film before discussing what makes the scene frightening and whether it's more or less frightening than traditional settings for horror stories, such as a graveyard.

Exploration

Tension building

To support differentiation in response to Activity 1 in the Student Book, first ask students to complete the 'Tension-building techniques' worksheet on Kerboodle.

Resources

Student Book 3: Activity 1, page 27

Kerboodle: 1.8 Tension-building techniques

Comparing tenses

To support differentiation and encourage careful evaluation in response to Activities 2a and 2b in the Student Book, ask students to complete the 'Comparing tenses' worksheet on Kerboodle.

Resources

Student Book 3: Activities 2a and 2b, page 27

Kerboodle: 1.8 Comparing tenses

Tense transformation

Hand out copies of the 'Tense transformation' worksheet on Kerboodle and ask students to practise transforming a past-tense extract from *My Swordhand is Singing* into the present tense. After they have completed that activity, ask them to compare how tense and dramatic the two versions are, before deciding which version of the extract they prefer.

Resources

Kerboodle: 1.8 Tense transformation

and guidance

Consolidation

Exploring narrative perspectives

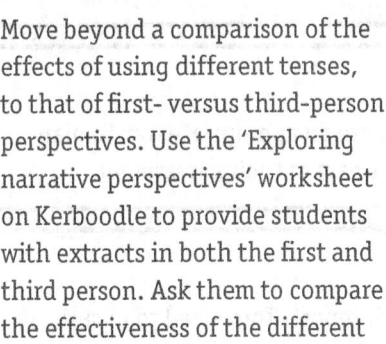

Move beyond a comparison of the effects of using different tenses, to that of first- versus third-person perspectives. Use the 'Exploring narrative perspectives' worksheet on Kerboodle to provide students with extracts in both the first and third person. Ask them to compare the effectiveness of the different extracts.

Resources
Kerboodle: 1.8 Exploring narrative perspectives

Characterization

Ask students to identify what is grammatically incorrect about the narrator's use of 'he don't let go' in the extract on page 26 of the Student Book. You could then ask them to make notes or discuss why the writer might have chosen to make the narrator use non-standard English. What does it suggest about him? How might it affect a reader's view of him?

Sinister science

Ask students to research an element of scientific study, such as genetic engineering or space travel, and devise a plot summary for a futuristic horror story incorporating elements of the science-fiction genre.

'The Tell-Tale Heart'

Ask students to read the extract from Edgar Allen Poe's classic horror story, 'The Tell-Tale Heart', on Kerboodle and then consider and explain how the punctuation is being used to reflect the narrator's state of mind.

Resources
Kerboodle: 1.8 'The Tell-Tale Heart' by Edgar Allen Poe

Ignite English interview

You might like to play Ignite Interview Film 2 to the class, in which Sarah Pinborough discusses structuring horror stories.

Resources
Kerboodle: 1 Ignite Interview Sarah Pinborough Film 2

Rating the tenses

Ask students to vote on which tense makes the horror genre more dramatic and tense – the past or the present. Invite volunteers to give reasons for their choices.

To survive or not to survive

Based on what they have learned about the character of Todd in the extract from *The Knife of Never Letting Go*, ask students to discuss and agree on whether or not he's likely to survive and why.

Progress Check

Use the 'Progress Check: self-evaluation' worksheet on Kerboodle to enable students to self-assess the accuracy and effectiveness of their own continuation of the Patrick Ness extract.

Resources
Kerboodle: 1.8 Progress Check: self-evaluation

Extra Time

Ask students to read Mary Shelley's *Frankenstein*, one of the first novels to create horror by drawing on fears for the future.

Assessment focus

Why are we assessing this?

Students have completed a unit on the horror genre. By studying many extracts and examples, they have had the opportunity to consider how horror writers use a range of techniques to frighten their readers. They have also practised key reading skills, such as inference and selecting textual evidence. This assessment gives them the opportunity to demonstrate the reading skills they have developed by writing a report which requires them to independently analyse, compare and evaluate three horror extracts.

What are students demonstrating?

Students will be able to:

- analyse, compare and evaluate three horror extracts
- select precise textual evidence to support points.

How to deliver the assessment

Suggestions and guidance on how to set up and prepare your students for the assessment are provided, as well as possible approaches to marking the assessment.

Alternative/additional assessment

There is an alternative end-of-unit assessment available on Kerboodle. This assessment leads to a written outcome and can be used either in addition to or instead of the Student Book end-of-unit assessment.

Resources

Kerboodle: 1.9 Alternative end-of-unit assessment

Assessment suggestions and guidance

Understanding the assessment

Check that students understand the assessment task set and the format in which you expect their report to be presented. Emphasize that they are being tested on their reading skills.

Resources

Student Book 3: pages 28–31

Planning

Remind students that they will need to choose an appropriate way to plan their work. They should include this plan as part of their assessment.

Completing the assessment

Remind students to edit and proofread their report. They need to ensure that they have expressed their ideas clearly, appropriately and accurately. Emphasize that students must complete the assessment individually, so that an accurate mark or level can be given.

Timing and writing expectation

Give students approximately two hours and expect between three and four A4 pages.

Marking

You will want to mark this in line with departmental and school marking guidelines. If you wish, you could use the Ignite English marking scales provided on Kerboodle. Using the Ignite English marking scales will help you to identify specific strengths and areas for improvement in an individual student's reading skills. This may help you to set development targets as well as building a profile of your class as readers.

Refer to the KS3 National Curriculum and Ignite English mapping grids on pages 154–156 of this Teacher Companion to identify other Ignite English units where these reading skills are covered, or ask students to use the SPAG interactives on Kerboodle to address any areas identified for improvement. The Grammar Reference Guide on Kerboodle contains definitions and additional examples of each of the spelling, punctuation and grammar points covered in the interactives, for your reference.

Resources

Kerboodle: 1 Ignite English marking scales

Kerboodle: SPAG interactives

Kerboodle: Grammar Reference Guide

Key for Kerboodle LRA resources   Worksheet   Interactive activity

Student Book answers

Below are the answers to any largely non-subjective Student Book activities contained within this unit.

Lesson 1

2   black, silvery, bronze, white, red

3   'vivid black shadow'; 'deserted'; 'A waiting stillness'; 'someone crouching to waylay me'; 'a shadowy corner'; 'twinge of apprehension'

Lesson 2

2b   'shut-up house'; 'batch of clouds'; 'broken chimneys and parapets'; 'unfamiliar queerness'; 'no human eye watched'; 'unwilling lock'; 'Dead air'; 'claw marks'; 'the cold hearth'

Lesson 3

1a   'without a single speck of colour about him anywhere'; 'with a strange intonation'; 'stood like a statue'; 'a strength which made me wince'; 'more like the hand of a dead than a living man'

1b   Courtly means in a formal manner, suitable for the royal court.

3   Notice that each paragraph ends with an action. Longer sentences build detail. The dash in the last sentence suggests a dramatic pause.

Lesson 4

1a   'tore'; 'rip'; 'crashed'; 'hammered'

Lesson 5

4a   The horror is that the man has asked for eternal life, but he has grown old and longs to lose this special gift.

4b   'beat me down'; 'marr'd and wasted me'; 'left me maim'd'; 'all I was in ashes'

4c   The moral is that we shouldn't tamper with the natural order of things.

Lesson 6

1a   'lumpy with boils and growths'; 'bright red blood dribbling from his mouth'; 'an ear hanging off'

1b   'It flapped as he waddled along'; 'as if he'd swallowed a desk lamp'

Lesson 8

1   Students could also find: use of present tense and repetition.

Unit 2: Relationships

Unit overview

Why are we teaching this?

How do the relationships that we have influence who we are? This unit will explore **ways in which relationships have been presented in texts** – with a particular focus on **poetry**. Students will consider parent–child relationships, as well as friendship and romantic love. They will also examine how the **context** of a text could influence, or be reflected by, the content. In addition, they will consider attitudes towards relationships in **literary fiction**, **non-fiction** and **song lyrics**.

The unit builds towards a GCSE-style comparison of pre-1914 poetry, as well as a creative-writing outcome. It aims to help students develop and practise the skills that they will need at this level.

What are the learning aims?

By the end of the unit, students will be able to:

- make links between texts and contexts
- analyse language and effect
- make clear personal responses to poetry
- understand the concept of courtly love
- compare poems.

How will this be assessed?

Key assessment task	Focus for assessment
Student Book: Writing a poem based on a relationship between two people.	<ul><li>Presenting ideas and feelings using literary language and poetic style.</li><li>Demonstrating quality of written communication.</li></ul>
Kerboodle: Reading and analysing a sonnet by Elizabeth Barrett Browning.	<ul><li>Commenting on theme and how the poet's viewpoint is presented in the poem.</li><li>Commenting on how the poem's form and structure helps to present the poet's thoughts and ideas.</li><li>Analysing how language and literary devices are used to communicate the poet's views, supporting ideas with relevant details from the text.</li></ul>

The end-of-unit assessment on Kerboodle can be used either instead of or in addition to the Student Book end-of-unit assessment.

Note that short Progress Checks also feature in this unit, providing formative assessment opportunities to support the students' learning.

Lesson sequence

This is a suggested lesson sequence, but you might choose to alter or add to it to suit your particular teaching needs.

Introducing the unit

1 First Relationships

- Consider and evaluate existing relationships.
- Respond to the Ignite Interview featuring Nick Cope.
- Develop an interpretation of a poem, exploring the use of figurative language.
- Explore the relationship presented in a poem.
- Analyse key aspects of language in a poem.

2 Mexican Bean	**3 Best Friends**	**4 Making Time**
• Analyse the use of imagery in conveying meaning to the reader. • Analyse the way in which parent–child relationships are presented in a poem. • Prepare a reading of a poem.	• Explore ideas and reflect on feelings through discussion with others. • Explore the concept of best friends, responding to ideas generated in a newspaper article. • Prepare for and argue a personal point of view.	• Explore how setting and dialogue can help to convey an author's message. • Consider a range of attitudes towards friendships. • Plan and prepare two contrasting role-plays.
5 The Wrong Clothes	**6 Loss**	**7 Without You**
• Understand how spoken language can reflect a character's background and social status. • Consider the presentation of friendship in literary fiction. • Explore the presentation of the relationship between Pip and Joe Gargery.	• Draw on knowledge, literary techniques, style and structure to draft a poem. • Read and analyse a poem about loss. • Write a poem about a friend or relative in a similar style.	• Explore how repetition and diversity of imagery can build up poetic structure. • Explore feelings of loss in a poem. • Write the next two stanzas of a poem.
8 Not a Fairy Tale Romance...	**9 Is Love Blind?**	**10 Assessment**
• Understand how traditional forms can be adapted to convey a contemporary message. • Consider the key ingredients of a traditional fairy tale. • Analyse a modern love poem with a focus on cliché.	• Compare texts written in the same literary tradition. • Understand the features of courtly love. • Make links between text and context.	• Student Book: Write a poem about a relationship between two people. • Kerboodle: Read and analyse a sonnet by Elizabeth Barrett Browning.

Preparing to teach

Refresh your knowledge

You might find it helpful to refer to the following key points when planning your teaching of this unit.

- Relationships are a very common theme in literature. They form one of the seven plots that are considered to make up all of literature. However, as well as romantic relationships, this unit also considers familial and friend relationships.

- The theme of relationships is evident not only in fiction but also in the real-world context, so students can incorporate and draw upon their own experiences in this unit.

- *The Epic of Gilgamesh* was written over 5000 years ago. It is a collection of epic poems about the unlikely friendship between the King – Gilgamesh – and Enkidu (the wild man created by the Gods as his equal). This tale has since been adapted and modernized in a number of different ways, including as a modern rap by Baba Brinkman (http://www.bababrinkman.com/music/#rapconteur).

Before deciding whether to play this rap version or not, you should listen to it in advance – to ensure that it's suitable for your students.

- The courtly love tradition was named in the 1880s, but it existed long before then. In this tradition, the lover has to prove his worth to his seemingly unattainable mistress by undertaking a series of noble acts and ordeals. Although based on sexual attraction, consummation of the relationship is not the goal. There were considered to be a number of specific stages to courtly love. The relationship between Romeo and Rosaline in *Romeo and Juliet* clearly demonstrates these features.

- In the literary tradition, the many examples of the use of the relationship theme include allegory – with religious imagery and human love being clearly connected.

Links and further reading

- The Poetry Archive (http://www.poetryarchive.org) is a one-stop shop for all things poetry. Not only does it contain useful information about a whole host of poets, but there are also recordings of many of the poets reading their own work. A children's archive (http://www.poetryarchive.org/childrensarchive) contains many of the same poems, as well as others more suitable for younger readers

- If you want to inspire and challenge students, look at Poetry By Heart – a national poetry recitation competition (http://www.poetrybyheart.org.uk/). This competition encourages students to get to grips with the language of poetry through learning it by heart. Even if you don't compete, it's a lovely varied resource.

- *Great Expectations* exists in a variety of film adaptations. Students could be asked to compare the presentation of Pip and Joe Gargery's relationship in the David Lean (1946) and Mike Newell (2012) versions.

- Students should be familiar with the fairy tale genre from their own childhood.

However, they are likely to be more aware of the sanitized Disney versions. The National Geographic Society has a website which allows you to choose from a variety of options to read the Grimm's versions, translated in 1914 (http://www.nationalgeographic.co.uk/grimm/main.html)

- Radio 4's *The Listening Project* (http://www.bbc.co.uk/radio4/features/the-listening-project) was designed to capture important conversations between ordinary individuals. The archive contains a wealth of material across a range of topics that would allow individual teachers or students to choose recordings that appeal to them. This resource could also be the inspiration for a more-extended extra time project, with students having conversations about issues that are important to them.

Please note that OUP is not responsible for third-party content. Although all links were correct at the time of publication, the content and location of this material may change.

Planning guidance and teaching tips

Think about how you can make the materials relevant to your students and responsive to their needs. Some suggested approaches to address key areas are provided below.

- In terms of the unit's themes, all students should find the material accessible.
- A **wide variety of poetry** has been included in the unit. However, there is scope to make use of the links opposite to select poems that are more to your own taste, as well as meeting the needs of your students.
- For **higher-achieving students**, the conceits in the works of poets such as John Donne might prove a fruitful area for study. The elaborate comparison in 'The Sun Rising', although potentially too explicit for some students, might prove interesting.
- For those students with **a more-cynical disposition**, consider Margaret Atwood's 'Siren Song', or many of the poems of Dorothy Parker. 'One Perfect Rose' would be an interesting jumping off point for a lesson about modern views of love.
- In this unit, students will explore the idea of **cliché** (considering how it's used in both literature and real life). Encouraging them to consider expressions that are overused to the point of being meaningless might help to improve the quality of their own writing!
- Many animated films are useful when considering cliché and parody, such as: *Shrek*, *Toy Story* and *Chicken Run*.
- In order to support students in developing the skills of **linking content to context**, poet fact files have been included for many of the poets.
- As students move towards GCSE study and beyond, they may be required to undertake **thematic study**. This unit helps to introduce the idea that one theme can be developed across a number of different texts and genres.
- Considering the **sonnet** and **elegy** forms will also help students to develop their skills as a prelude to their GCSE studies.
- One of the issues considered in this unit is the idea of **friendship**. In the age of social media, many students will have large **online social networks**, which are worth giving some consideration to (with a focus on the notion of 'friends' and what a 'friend' means in the 21st century). For many students, online social networks are a key part of their relationships with others, so considering platforms such as Facebook and Twitter is a worthwhile activity. Teachers unfamiliar with these concepts will find that students are more than willing to share their expertise!
- For some students, personal relationships may be a difficult subject, so teachers will need to use their professional judgement and knowledge of the class to make appropriate selections of resources and activities.
- Many students may find the older poetry challenging. Where they have difficulties with the language, they should be encouraged to work out the meanings of unfamiliar words from the context, although some of the more-difficult vocabulary has been glossed.
- Refer to the **Grammar Reference Guide** on Kerboodle for definitions and exemplars of the specific grammar and punctuation terms covered in this unit.

Lesson focus

Why are we teaching this?

As an introduction to the theme of relationships, students consider their earliest relationships and begin to explore the idea that relationships are not always clear-cut. They also consider writers' use of language and its impact.

What are students learning?

Students will be able to:

● develop an interpretation of a poem, exploring the use of figurative language.

How you could teach this

A variety of activities and approaches are provided on the right for you to select from and adapt to meet the needs of your students. The Kerboodle lesson player sequence is derived from these suggestions, to act as a starting point for your lesson.

Answers

Answers to Student Book activities, where relevant, can be found on page 61.

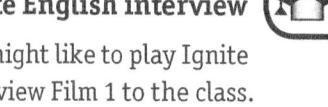

Teaching suggestions

Ignition

Ignite English interview

You might like to play Ignite Interview Film 1 to the class. In this film we are introduced to Nick Cope, songwriter and performer, and his thoughts about relationships.

Resources
Kerboodle: 2 Ignite Interview Nick Cope Film 1

Connections

Ask students to respond to Activity 1 in the Student Book by drawing a diagram showing their relationships with other people. They should then discuss with a partner someone who plays an important part in their life. Encourage students to choose a relationship with someone other than their parents or siblings to discuss with their partner.

Resources
Student Book 3: Activities 1 and 2, page 33

Considering relationships

Ask students to think about their relationships with their parents or carers and then list the things they agree and disagree about. Be sensitive that some students may be involved in major conflict with their parents or carers.

Resources
Student Book 3: Activity 1, page 34

Exploration

'Mother Any Distance'

Ask students to read and respond to the Simon Armitage poem on page 35 of the Student Book. Encourage them to consider both literal and figurative meaning in the poem. Ensure that they understand the difference between the terms 'literal' and 'figurative'. It helps to link the word 'figure' with the word 'image' or 'imagery', and to discuss how pictures conjure up moods and feelings.

Resources
Student Book 3: Activities 2–4, pages 34–35

Imagery in 'Mother Any Distance'

Use the image gallery on Kerboodle to illustrate a series of images used in 'Mother Any Distance'. You could do this even before reading the poem. Ask students to share their immediate thoughts/feelings about what the images evoke.

Resources
Kerboodle: 2.1 Imagery in 'Mother Any Distance'

and guidance

Consolidation

Falling or flying

Simon Armitage's poem tries to express through imagery the tension between being held back (falling, with the security of what we may fall back to) and being free (flying). Discuss how space walking, kites and anchors all represent aspects of this tension. Students could use the 'Falling or flying imagery' worksheet on Kerboodle to identify how mothers both anchor us and let us fly.

Resources

Kerboodle: 2.1 Falling or flying imagery

'Anchor. Kite.'

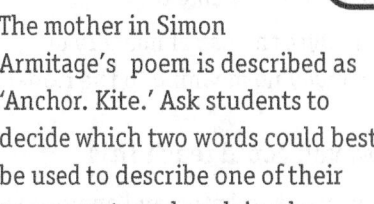

Support Activity 4 in the Student Book by asking students to focus on the choice of imagery in 'Mother Any Distance' – in particular, 'Anchor. Kite.' Explain that students should try to analyse the poet's intentions in relation to this imagery. You could use the 'Anchor. Kite.' imagery worksheet on Kerboodle to help scaffold students' responses.

Resources

Student Book 3: Activity 4, page 35

Kerboodle: 2.1 'Anchor. Kite.' imagery

'Catrin'

Ask students to read the Gillian Clark poem 'Catrin', supplied on Kerboodle, and consider how the relationship between mother and child is presented within the poem. Ask whether they can name three key differences between the relationship in 'Catrin' and the relationship in 'Mother Any Distance'.

Resources

Kerboodle: 2.1 'Catrin' by Gillian Clark

A letter to ...

Ask students to write a letter to one of the significant adults in their lives, explaining what they mean to them. The 'A letter to ...' worksheet on Kerboodle could be used to support students as required. (As an alternative, you could suggest to higher-achieving students that they emulate Simon Armitage by writing a poem instead.)

Resources

Kerboodle: 2.1 A letter to ...

Extra Time

Ask students to write a tweet, of no more than 140 characters, in which they explore their relationship with their parents.

Write a title

Ask students to write an alternative title for the Armitage poem and then explain their thinking.

Parental imagery

The mother in Simon Armitage's poem is described as 'Anchor. Kite.' Ask students to decide which two words could best be used to describe one of their own parents and explain why.

Relationships diagram

Ask students to revisit Activity 1 on page 33 of the Student Book by reconsidering the connections they have with people in their own lives. This should take the form of a diagram that shows not only the distance between them but also the significant elements of each relationship. If a simpler exercise would be more appropriate, this activity could be restricted to family members only – using the 'Family relationships' worksheet on Kerboodle.

Resources

Student Book 3: Activity 1, page 33

Kerboodle: 2.1 Family relationships

 Weblink   Presentation Interactive activity

Lesson focus

Why are we teaching this?

In this lesson, students explore the complicated relationships between parents and their children, using a Sylvia Plath poem (in particular, the metaphors and similes used to describe and evoke the relationship). Imagery is a key lens through which poetry is studied and appreciated, so this lesson builds on the imagery work of the previous lesson.

What are students learning?

Students will be able to:

- analyse the use of imagery in conveying meaning to the reader.

How you could teach this

A variety of activities and approaches are provided on the right for you to select from and adapt to meet the needs of your students. The Kerboodle lesson player sequence is derived from these suggestions, to act as a starting point for your lesson.

Answers

Answers to Student Book activities, where relevant, can be found on page 61.

Teaching suggestions

Ignition

Like a ...

Show students a short film clip of a baby moving in the womb (search on YouTube for a suitable clip, using the key words 'baby moving in womb'). Encourage students to call out the names of animals, vegetables or even inanimate objects that it reminds them of, however fleetingly, as it plays.

When I was a baby ...

What do students know about themselves when they were very young? Ask for volunteers to tell the class something about themselves that other students might not be aware of. Model some suggestions based on your own life to get students started.

What am I?

In response to Activity 1 in the Student Book, ask students to read the Sylvia Plath poem 'You're' and identify the poem's subject. To help them understand the meaning and structure of the poem, suggest that students put the title word before all the images that Plath describes.

Resources
Student Book: Activity 1, page 36

Exploration

Metaphors and similes

As an introduction to Activity 2 in the Student Book, write a metaphor on the whiteboard and ask students for a quick definition. Do the same with a simile. Read out (or make up) some images – each time asking for a quick class vote on whether it's a metaphor or a simile.

Resources
Student Book 3: Activity 2, page 36

Make a link

Poets can be very inventive with the links that they make. See if students can be just as inventive in the following game. Explain that, working in pairs, one student has to name an object. Their partner then has to think of a way in which a baby could be described as like an aspect of that object. For example: 'A desk lamp.' 'Its face lights up when it sees Mother.' Give praise for the most inventive links suggested in subsequent whole-class feedback.

Draw the image

Students who are more visually gifted could be asked to draw one or more of the images used by Sylvia Plath in 'You're', and then to explain how the image reflects the description or mood intended by the poet.

and guidance

Consolidation

'Morning song'

For comparison/extension, you could ask students to read and respond to the poem 'Morning Song', also by Sylvia Plath, by asking them to consider the relationship portrayed in the poem between the mother and her child. The text of the poem has been supplied on Kerboodle.

Resources
Kerboodle: 2.2 'Morning Song' by Sylvia Plath

'Babysitting'

For further comparison/ extension, students could also be asked to consider the presentation of the relationship in Gillian Clark's poem 'Babysitting' (also supplied on Kerboodle).

Resources
Kerboodle: 2.2 'Babysitting' by Gillian Clark

Using hyphens

In support of Activity 3 in the Student Book, you could use the Grammar Reference Guide on Kerboodle to strengthen students' understanding of hyphens.

Resources
Student Book 3: Activity 3, page 36

Kerboodle: Grammar Reference Guide (hyphen)

How does she feel?

Provide the following possible answers to Activity 4 in the Student Book: curious, anxious, joyful, loving, amazed, interested. Ask students, working in pairs, to choose the one feeling word that they agree with the most, and then to identify three pieces of evidence from the poem to back up their choice.

Resources
Student Book 3: Activity 4, page 36

Extra Time

Ask students to use the weblink below to read the poem 'Born Yesterday: For Sally Amis' by Phillip Larkin, which was written for the newborn daughter of his friend Kingsley Amis. Then ask them to imagine that they are adults themselves and to write their own wishes for their children. You could offer them the choice of writing in either poetic or narrative form.

Resources
Weblink: http://www.martinamisweb.com/pre_2006/yesterday.htm

Made-up words

Plath often made up new words by hyphenating old ones to enhance and clarify their poetic meaning. Ask students to use hyphenated words, in the style of Plath, to write a description of themselves.

Recitation

Ask students, working in pairs or small groups, to prepare a recitation of 'You're' – paying particular attention to the sound patterns used by Plath to help them understand the poem more effectively.

Resources
Student Book 3: Activity 5, page 37

Language of love?

Ask students to consider the language used as a whole by Sylvia Plath in 'You're' to explore the poet's love for her child. The worksheet provided on Kerboodle offers pointers for consideration. Encourage students to create their own 'love scale' and to decide what the language used reveals about the poet's feelings.

Resources
Kerboodle: 2.2 Analysing Plath's imagery

Weblink   Presentation   Interactive activity

Lesson focus

Why are we teaching this?

In this lesson, students move from an exploration of parent–child relationships to that of close friendships. They will use the opinions expressed in a newspaper article to stimulate a class debate about best friends – practising organising their ideas and sharing them in a persuasive way in the debate.

What are students learning?

Students will be able to:

● explore ideas and reflect on feelings through discussion with others.

How you could teach this

A variety of activities and approaches are provided on the right for you to select from and adapt to meet the needs of your students. The Kerboodle lesson player sequence is derived from these suggestions, to act as a starting point for your lesson.

Answers

Answers to Student Book activities, where relevant, can be found on page 61.

Teaching suggestions

Ignition

First best friend

Support Activity 1 in the Student Book by asking students, working in pairs, to discuss what they remember about their first best friend. Be sensitive to the possibility that some students might get caught up in some uncomfortable feelings/memories – especially if their experience of friendship has been difficult.

Resources
Student Book 3: Activity 1, page 38

'Three'

Read out the poem 'Three' from the Student Book. Then ask students for their comments about what the poem says about best friends (e.g. they fall out; they can be replaced temporarily; they are not always mutual; there's a funny side to the need to have a best friend).

Acrostic

Ask students to use the letters in the phrase 'best friend' to write an acrostic poem about either their best friend, or what they think a best friend should be like.

Exploration

Unfamiliar words

To help students think about the meaning of unfamiliar words in the newspaper article, you could give them the 'Understanding unfamiliar words' worksheet on Kerboodle to complete.

Resources
Student Book 3: Activity 2a, page 38

Kerboodle: 2.3 Understanding unfamiliar words

Continuum line

After they have read the newspaper article in the Student Book, you could ask students to position themselves along a continuum line, according to how much they agree or disagree with the idea put forward in the article that children shouldn't have best friends. Ask a selection of students to explain their positions.

Write to reply

As initial preparation for Activity 3a in the Student Book, ask students to write a letter to the headmaster referred to in the article, giving their personal opinions about the views he has expressed (with some reasoned argument to support their thoughts).

Resources
Student Book 3: Activity 3a, page 38

Key for Kerboodle LRA resources   Lesson Player   Image   Video    Worksheet

and guidance

Consolidation

Debate

Continue the preparation for the debate by dividing the class into two groups: those in favour of banning best friends and those against. Ask them to work in small groups to collate their ideas – using research skills to ensure that their arguments are well supported.

Resources
Student Book 3: Activity 3a, page 38

Organizing ideas

You could suggest that students use the 'Debate – organizing ideas' worksheet on Kerboodle to help them arrange and focus their ideas before actually speaking in the class debate.

Resources
Student Book 3: Activity 3a, page 38

Kerboodle: 2.3 Debate – organizing ideas

Focus on speaking

In advance of the class debate, give students some advice about developing their speaking skills. Ask them which tone would be good for them to adopt in the debate. Also remind them that they can use hand gestures and facial expressions when public speaking. You could also ask students to work in pairs and complete a peer progress check – giving one suggestion and some praise after each practice.

Resources
Student Book 3: Activity 3a, page 38

Progress Check

If you use the Progress Check suggestion in the Student Book, the worksheet on Kerboodle will provide a template for students' responses. You could also ask students to include a target for future improvement.

Resources
Student Book 3: Progress Check, page 39

Kerboodle: 2.3 Debate Progress Check

Debate: Beat the teacher

Present some arguments in favour of banning best friends and ask the class to present some arguments against. This debate could be organized so that you make a point and then a student is chosen to respond. By taking it in turns, either the class or the teacher will win the debate – depending on which side runs out of ideas first.

Best friend guide

Ask students to write a guide to being a best friend – thinking about the skills and qualities that a best friend should have.

Extra Time

Ask students to create the publicity material for a social media event, with the aim of meeting and making new friends. Emphasize that they must consider the language and presentation of the publicity material carefully.

Lesson focus

Why are we teaching this?

Continuing the theme introduced in the last lesson, students now consider different aspects of friendship in more detail – developing their understanding of different points of view and demonstrating this through contrasting short role-plays.

What are students learning?

Students will be able to:

- explore how setting and dialogue can help to convey an author's message.

How you could teach this

A variety of activities and approaches are provided on the right for you to select from and adapt to meet the needs of your students. The Kerboodle lesson player sequence is derived from these suggestions, to act as a starting point for your lesson.

Answers

Answers to Student Book activities, where relevant, can be found on page 61.

Teaching suggestions

Ignition

What are friends for?

Ask students to discuss in pairs what friends are for. Guide them to identify the qualities that they consider important in friends. Using the 'Friends and friendship' interactive activity on Kerboodle, ask the class to rank the friendship qualities in order of importance. Conduct a whole-class feedback to compile the best ideas and reach a consensus.

Resources
Kerboodle: 2.4 Friends and friendship

Imaginary friend

Encourage students to think back to their early childhood. Did they have an imaginary friend? What was this friend like? Why do they think that young children often have imaginary friends?

Dictionary definition

Ask students to write a definition of the word 'friend' – explaining what it means to them. You could then ask them to compare their definition with one in a dictionary (considering similarities and differences between the two).

Ignite English interview

You might like to play Ignite Interview Film 2 to the class, in which Nick Cope discusses writing and editing.

Resources
Kerboodle: 2 Ignite Interview Nick Cope Film 2

Exploration

Attitudes to friendship

You could extend Activity 1 in the Student Book by asking students to discuss a series of quotations about friendship. Use the 'Attitudes to friendship' presentation on Kerboodle to show each quotation in turn – asking for a quick show of hands to indicate whether students agree or disagree with it. Follow up each show of hands by asking two students to explain why they either agreed or disagreed with the quotation.

Resources
Student Book 3: Activity 1, page 40

Kerboodle: 2.4 Attitudes to friendship

Friendly images

Show the 'Images of friendship' image gallery on Kerboodle and ask students to discuss, in pairs, which aspect of friendship shines through the most in each case. Is this an aspect that matters to them? You could then ask students, working individually or in pairs, to write down the different characteristics/aspects of friendship and rank them in order of importance, before feeding back to the class.

Resources
Kerboodle: 2.4 Images of friendship

and guidance

Consolidation

'A Time to Talk'

When discussing Robert Frost's poem, 'A Time to Talk', in response to Activities 2a and 2b in the Student Book, point out that the poet describes in detail what he doesn't do, as well as what he does do. Ask students what they think the purpose and effect of this detail is. (Expect them to approve of the poet's attitude towards his friend.) Then ask them to consider times when stopping to talk may not always be the best policy.

Resources
Student Book 3: Activities 2a and 2b, page 41

Role-play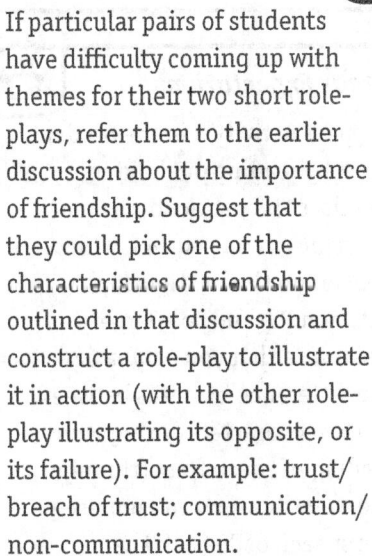

If particular pairs of students have difficulty coming up with themes for their two short role-plays, refer them to the earlier discussion about the importance of friendship. Suggest that they could pick one of the characteristics of friendship outlined in that discussion and construct a role-play to illustrate it in action (with the other role-play illustrating its opposite, or its failure). For example: trust/breach of trust; communication/non-communication.

Resources
Student Book 3: Activity 3, page 41

'A Poison Tree'

For comparison/extension, you could ask students to read the William Blake poem 'A Poison Tree', provided on Kerboodle, and consider the poet's attitude towards relationships. In particular, focus on the way in which language is used to present his ideas.

Resources
Kerboodle: 2.4 'A Poison Tree' by William Blake

'Brendon Gallacher'

For further comparison/extension, you could also ask students to read Jackie Kay's poem 'Brendon Gallacher' (provided on Kerboodle) – analysing the way in which friendship is presented there. A lot of material about this poem is available on BBC Bitesize (http://www.bbc.co.uk/bitesize/) – search using the key words 'Brendon Gallacher'.

Resources
Kerboodle: 2.4 'Brendon Gallacher' by Jackie Kay

Extra Time

Ask students to write an explanation of how one of the poets whose work has been covered in the lesson presents ideas about friendships, and what effect this has on the reader.

What's the message?

As the pairs act out their scenes, ask the audience to consider one word or phrase that they think best describes the attitude towards friendship being displayed in that particular role-play. Ask for volunteers to share their ideas before moving on to the next role-play.

Resources
Student Book 3: Activity 3 and Progress Check, page 41

Progress Check

If desired, a worksheet is available on Kerboodle to provide a template for the peer-based Progress Check in the Student Book.

Resources
Student Book 3: Progress Check, page 41

Kerboodle: 2.4 Role-plays Progress Check

Dear friend ...

Ask students to write a short email or text to a friend to whom they have not actually spoken for a while – either real or imaginary – telling them something that they would like to have more time to discuss properly.

Lesson focus

Why are we teaching this?

In this lesson, students continue thinking about relationships between friends – this time as presented in literary fiction. The emphasis is on how status affects friendships. The lesson provides an opportunity to analyse how writers convey information about character through dialogue.

What are students learning?

Students will be able to:

- understand how spoken language can reflect a character's background and social status.

How you could teach this

A variety of activities and approaches are provided on the right for you to select from and adapt to meet the needs of your students. The Kerboodle lesson player sequence is derived from these suggestions, to act as a starting point for your lesson.

Answers

Answers to Student Book activities, where relevant, can be found on page 61.

Teaching suggestions

Ignition

Unlikely friends

Look for 'unlikely friendships' in a search engine, which should bring up a series of animal images/videos. Ask students to consider what it is about the differences between the animals that (a) might work well (how they might benefit from each other) and (b) might not work well (what difficulties the differences might cause).

Friendships in literature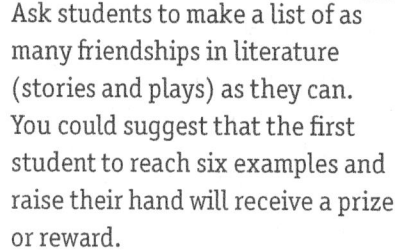

Ask students to make a list of as many friendships in literature (stories and plays) as they can. You could suggest that the first student to reach six examples and raise their hand will receive a prize or reward.

Resources
Student Book 3: Activity 1, page 42

Real friends?

Ask students to think about their online social networks and make a list of the categories of 'friends' that they have. Ask them to consider what difference there might be between a 'friend' and an 'online friend'.

Exploration

Why talk about friendship?

Ask students to discuss why they think friendship is such an important theme in literature and film. Encourage them to think about the wider idea of friendship, as well as specific examples.

Resources
Student Book 3: Activity 2, page 42

Gilgamesh

Show the short clip from *Star Trek: The Next Generation* in which the story of Gilgamesh and Enkidu is described (search on YouTube, using the key words 'Gilgamesh' and 'Star Trek'). Ask students what it is about the story that captures the imagination.

Great Expectations

Support Activity 3 in the Student Book by reading out loud to the class the extract from *Great Expectations* on page 43, which focuses on the relationship between Pip and Joe Gargery. Make sure that you emphasize the difference in status between the two characters during your reading of the extract (through the ways in which you represent the speech of Joe and the narrative of Pip).

Resources
Student Book 3: Activity 3, page 43

and guidance

Informality and dialect

You could further support Activity 3 by providing examples to ensure that students know what the terms 'informality' and 'dialect' mean. The 'Informality and dialect' worksheet on Kerboodle will help to consolidate students' understanding. The first paragraph of the Student Book extract (Joe's speech) has also been provided as a separate presentation, which could be annotated to emphasize key examples in the text (two examples have already been annotated).

Resources

Student Book 3: Activity 3, page 43

Kerboodle: 2.5 Informality and dialect

Kerboodle: 2.5 Joe Gargery's speech

Images of Joe

Show the class some online images of Joe Gargery from various performances of *Great Expectations* (an online search using his name will bring up numerous possibilities). Conduct a class vote to decide which image students think best displays the 'simple dignity' described in the Student Book extract.

What does he mean?

To help lower-achieving students with Activity 4 in the Student Book, you could give them the 'What does Joe Gargery mean?' worksheet on Kerboodle, which provides three different answer options. Ask them to discuss in pairs which answer option they think best explains what Joe Gargery means in the first paragraph of the Student Book extract – offering evidence from Joe's speech to support their decision.

Resources

Student Book 3: Activity 4, page 43

Kerboodle: 2.5 What does Joe Gargery mean?

George and Lennie

Ask students to read the short extract from John Steinbeck's *Of Mice and Men* provided on Kerboodle. Encourage them to consider what kind of friendship George and Lennie have – and to explain how they can tell this from the extract.

Resources

Kerboodle: 2.5 *Of Mice and Men* extract

Three things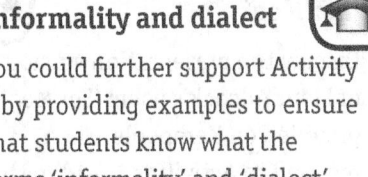

Ask students, working individually, to write down three things that they have learned about Pip from the Student Book extract. Then discuss as a class.

Resources

Student Book 3: Activity 5, page 43

A friend to lean on

Ask students to read the short extract from Tolkien's *The Fellowship of the Ring*, provided on Kerboodle. Then discuss whether students think that there is such a thing as being too loyal to a friend. Why?

Resources

Kerboodle: 2.5 Tolkien extract

A letter to Joe

Ask students, working in role as Pip, to write to Joe Gargery responding to his criticisms and explaining how they intend to change.

Extra Time

Ask students to read through their Activity 6 writing pieces and make improvements. Encourage them to check their spelling, punctuation and grammar.

Lesson focus

Why are we teaching this?

One of the best ways of learning about literary techniques, style and structure is to use them in creative composition. This lesson builds on students' poetry-reading skills, by requiring them to write a poem on a similar theme. It also introduces a new aspect of relationships – the loss of someone close.

What are students learning?

Students will be able to:

- draw on knowledge, literary techniques, style and structure to draft a poem.

How you could teach this

A variety of activities and approaches are provided on the right for you to select from and adapt to meet the needs of your students. The Kerboodle lesson player sequence is derived from these suggestions, to act as a starting point for your lesson.

Answers

Answers to Student Book activities, where relevant, can be found on page 61.

Teaching suggestions

Ignition

It is better …

Give students the statement: 'It is better to have loved and lost than never to have loved at all.' Then ask them to position themselves along a continuum line – according to how much they agree or disagree with this statement. Complete the activity by asking several students to explain the reasons why they positioned themselves where they did.

Recalling memories

Ask students to recall a memory of being with someone or something (relative, friend or pet) who is no longer with them (having moved away or died). Ask them to rate what they feel about the memory on a spectrum from 'very sad' to 'very happy' (which could be arranged as a continuum line across the classroom, or done as a show of hands). If volunteers are willing to talk about their memories, you could take some feedback, but you must be sensitive to recent or painful losses in this and the other activities in this lesson.

'Break, break, break'

Read the poem 'Break, break, break' by Alfred, Lord Tennyson (supplied on Kerboodle) with the class. Ask students to consider the mood of the poem. You could also ask higher-achieving students to discuss what they think might have prompted Tennyson to write this poem.

Resources
Kerboodle: 2.6 'Break, break, break' by Tennyson

Exploration

'For Meg'

Display the presentation version of Fleur Adcock's poem 'For Meg', provided on Kerboodle. Then respond to Activities 1a–1d in the Student Book by annotating it as a whole-class activity. Identify the theme of the poem, as well as how this theme has been presented through the poet's choice of language.

Resources

Student Book 3: Activities 1a–1d, page 44

Kerboodle: 2.6 'For Meg' by Fleur Adcock

Elegy

Introduce and discuss the term 'elegy' (a mourning poem). 'Tichborne's Elegy', written in 1586 and supplied on Kerboodle, is an accessible and moving literary heritage text that you could use for further analysis and/or comparison with 'For Meg'.

Resources
Kerboodle: 2.6 'Tichborne's Elegy' by Chidiock Tichborne

and guidance

Consolidation

'Adonais'

Following the elegy activity above, you could ask higher-achieving students to use 'Adonais' worksheets 1 and 2, provided on Kerboodle, to analyse the way in which the relationship between the poet (Shelley) and his subject (Keats) has been presented in the first three stanzas of the poem (which consists of 55 stanzas in total).

Resources

Kerboodle: 2.6 'Adonais' worksheet 1

Kerboodle: 2.6 'Adonais' worksheet 2

Drafting a poem

When briefing students for Activity 2 in the Student Book, make it clear that the person they write about can still be very much alive! You could suggest that students use the 'Drafting a poem' worksheet on Kerboodle to help them plan their ideas.

Resources

Student Book 3: Activity 2, page 44

Kerboodle: 2.6 Drafting a poem

Editing and proofreading

Use the Progress Check activity in the Student Book as an opportunity to emphasize the importance of editing and proofreading creative work. Explain that when each student receives their partner's suggestions for improvement, they should use them to review the whole poem, make changes (edit) and then check the whole piece (proofread).

Resources

Student Book 3: Progress Check, page 44

Mourning

Ask students to read the extract from *Ways to Live Forever* by Sally Nicholls, provided on Kerboodle, and discuss the different methods described within it for dealing with the death of a loved one. They could then go on to discuss what they are able to infer about each culture from this information.

Resources

Kerboodle: 2.6 *Ways to Live Forever* extract

Extra Time

Based on the work carried out in this lesson, ask students to write a text about missing someone. Say that it could be in the form of a letter, a poem, a diary entry or a song.

Recitation

Ask volunteers to read out their poems from Activity 2 in the Student Book. Then ask the rest of the class to vote on the best ones by considering (a) the content and style and (b) the quality of the performance.

Writing an elegy

Ask students to choose a person, pet or object about which to write an elegy. Explain that they can take either a serious or a humorous approach in their writing. If appropriate, offer students the 'Writing an elegy' worksheet on Kerboodle to help them.

Resources

Kerboodle: 2.6 Writing an elegy

'Stop All the Clocks'

Use the weblink below to play the class a short BBC video clip of W. H. Auden's poem known as 'Stop All the Clocks' being recited to an accompanying video background. After playing the clip, ask students to discuss how they think the poet felt about the person in the poem.

Resources

Weblink: http://www.bbc.co.uk/learningzone/clips/w-h-auden-stop-all-the-clocks-poem-only/1318.html

 Weblink   Presentation   Interactive activity

Lesson focus

Why are we teaching this?

In this lesson, students will explore ways in which the poet Adrian Henri expresses his views about relationships through two poems, in particular by analysing the poem 'Without You' and its impact on the reader.

What are students learning?

Students will be able to:

- explore how repetition and diversity of imagery can build up poetic structure.

How you could teach this

A variety of activities and approaches are provided on the right for you to select from and adapt to meet the needs of your students. The Kerboodle lesson player sequence is derived from these suggestions, to act as a starting point for your lesson.

Teaching suggestions

Ignition

I care

Encourage students to discuss how it feels to be apart from someone they love. Be sensitive to any recent losses experienced by members of the class.

Resources
Student Book 3: Activity 1, page 46

Without my ...

Ask students to consider an object that they couldn't live without, and then to describe it through a list of five of its features that are vital to them. However, they must not reveal what it is – it is up to the rest of the class to guess!

'No man is an island'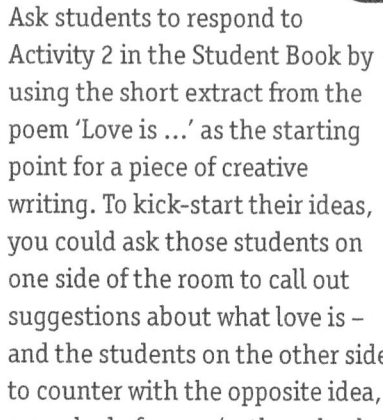

Get students to write the phrase 'No man is an island' in the middle of a page and brainstorm what they think it means. Encourage them to draw on their previous work from this unit to add ideas.

Exploration

Love is ...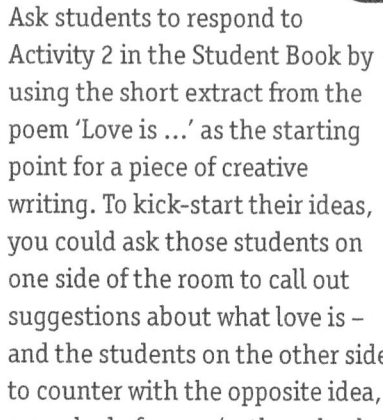

Ask students to respond to Activity 2 in the Student Book by using the short extract from the poem 'Love is ...' as the starting point for a piece of creative writing. To kick-start their ideas, you could ask those students on one side of the room to call out suggestions about what love is – and the students on the other side to counter with the opposite idea, e.g. a bed of roses / a thorn bush.

Resources
Student Book 3: Activity 2, page 46

'Without You'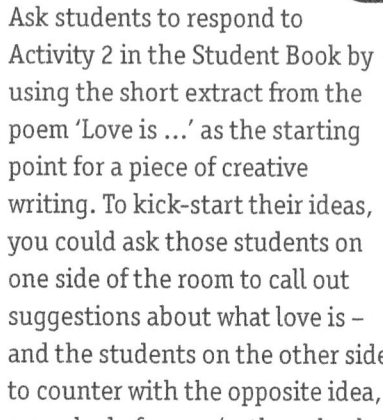

Ask students to read the Adrian Henri poem 'Without You' on page 47 of the Student Book and consider to whom the poet is addressing the poem – providing evidence to support their ideas. If necessary, you could suggest that students read the 'Using evidence' worksheet on Kerboodle to remind them about the key points of citing textual evidence when answering questions.

Resources
Student Book 3: Activity 3, page 46

Kerboodle: 2.7 Using evidence

Answers

Answers to Student Book activities, where relevant, can be found on page 61.

and guidance

Artist and poet

Use the weblink below to show the class some of Adrian Henri's paintings. Ask what light they appear to throw on the kind of person he was. What links can students find, if any, between the images in his paintings and those in 'Without You'?

Resources
Weblink: http://www.adrian henri.com/

Draw an image

You could follow up Activity 5 in the Student Book by inviting students to choose an image from 'Without You' to draw or paint – emphasizing through their artwork the meaning that they believe Henri intended by using that particular image.

Resources
Student Book 3: Activity 5, page 46

With you

The poem 'Without You' focuses on what life would be like without this person who means so much to the poet. Ask students to choose a section of the poem and then to rewrite it – beginning each line 'With you ...', and providing a vivid image of what life is like with that person. Provide an example, e.g. the first line could be rewritten as: 'With you every morning feels like a long weekend'. Students could then explore what difference this new perspective makes to the emotional impact of the poem.

Repetition

Play the class Fleetwood Mac's song 'Without You', and ask students to consider what the repetition of the phrase gives to the song. Discuss whether the repetition of the same phrase in Henri's poem has a similar or different effect – and why. The discussion could then widen into the similarities/differences between poetry and song.

Consolidation

Recitation

Ask students, working in pairs, to read each other their poems from Activity 2 in the Student Book and provide feedback on the use of repetition and imagery.

Nothing Compares 2U

Show the class the video of Sinead O'Connor's song *Nothing Compares 2U* (which can be found on YouTube). Ask students to consider how the visual imagery in the video is used to support the meaning of the lyrics.

Obituary

Show the presentation on Kerboodle and ask students to focus on what the language being used in each obituary demonstrates about the writer's opinion of the person who has just died.

Resources
Kerboodle: 2.7 Contrasting obituaries

Extra Time

Ask students to analyse the eulogy given by Earl Spencer at Princess Diana's funeral – with a focus on how he presents both his and the nation's feelings. The weblink below provides both a video and transcript.

Resources
Weblink: www.american rhetoric.com/speeches/9th earlspencerdianaeulogy.htm

Lesson focus

Why are we teaching this?

In this lesson, students will develop an understanding of how traditional genres, such as fairy tales, can be adapted and employed to suit new purposes and audiences. They will also examine the use of clichés in more detail.

What are students learning?

Students will be able to:

● understand how traditional forms can be adapted to convey a contemporary message.

How you could teach this

A variety of activities and approaches are provided on the right for you to select from and adapt to meet the needs of your students. The Kerboodle lesson player sequence is derived from these suggestions, to act as a starting point for your lesson.

Teaching suggestions

Ignition

Fairy tales

In response to Activity 1 in the Student Book, guide students to list the key ingredients of a traditional fairy tale. Then use their lists as the basis for a short discussion about the conventions of the genre.

Resources
Student Book 3: Activity 1, page 48

Cliché central

As preparation for Activities 4a and 4b in the Student Book, make sure that students know what a cliché is and then ask them to make a list of as many as they can. You could choose a particular situation to help them focus their thoughts, such as school clichés.

Ranking clichés

Ask students to look at the 'Ranking clichés' worksheet on Kerboodle and rank the clichés in the table according to how clichéd they think they are.

Resources
Kerboodle: 2.8 Ranking clichés

Exploration

The world of cliché

Give students the 'Clichéd texts' worksheet on Kerboodle and ask them to read the two texts and highlight or underline the clichés they contain. You could then discuss during feedback whether each cliché serves a useful purpose or not.

Resources
Kerboodle: 2.8 Clichéd texts

Two fairy tales

If students need help completing Activity 2 in the Student Book, because they have scant knowledge about the plots of the two Grimm's fairy tales on which Liz Lochhead's poem is based (Rapunzel and Rumpelstiltskin), you could omit this particular Student Book activity and ask students to read the 'Two Grimm's fairy tales' information worksheet on Kerboodle instead. This provides a short plot summary of each fairy tale and would also be useful when students are responding to Activity 3 in the Student Book.

Resources
Student Book 3: Activities 2 and 3, page 48

Kerboodle: 2.8 Two Grimm's fairy tales

Answers

Answers to Student Book activities, where relevant, can be found on page 61.

and guidance

Consolidation

'Rapunzelstiltskin'

Ask students to read the text of 'Rapunzelstiltskin' on page 49 of the Student Book and consider Liz Lochhead's more-modern view of relationships. If required, the 'Rapunzelstiltskin' worksheet on Kerboodle will provide some scaffolding support for lower-achieving students.

Resources

Student Book 3: Activities 3, 4a and 4b, page 48

Kerboodle: 2.8 'Rapunzelstiltskin'

'I Wanna Be Yours'

Ask students to read John Cooper Clarke's poem 'I Wanna Be Yours' on the Kerboodle worksheet and then answer the accompanying questions. These questions ask students to make a personal response to the poem, with a focus on the shift in tone at the end.

Resources

Kerboodle: 2.8 'I Wanna Be Yours' by John Cooper Clarke

Fairy tale parody

Use the weblink below to show students an extract from a parody of a fairy tale ('Little Red Riding Hood' from *Politically Correct Bedtime Stories*). Then challenge them to write their own parody (of the same fairy tale, or any other fairy tale of their choice).

Resources

Weblink: http://www.jamesfinngarner.com/pdf/PCBS_excerpt.pdf

Robin Hood

Ask students what they expect of the character Robin Hood. Then show a YouTube clip of Robin Hood and his Merry Men from *Shrek* and ask students to discuss the differences between their expectations of Robin Hood and this version.

'Two Cures For Love'

Ask students to read Wendy Cope's poem 'Two Cures For Love' on the Kerboodle worksheet and then answer the accompanying questions, which ask them to consider Cope's view of romantic relationships.

Resources

Kerboodle: 2.8 'Two Cures For Love' by Wendy Cope

School reports

Challenge students to write a school report about themselves in which they employ excessive use of cliché. Explain that they then have to write a second school report that is more meaningful.

'Flowers'

Use the weblink below to read or play students Wendy Cope's poem 'Flowers'. Discuss whether it is better to have nearly bought flowers or to have not thought about buying them.

Resources

Weblink: http://www.poetryarchive.org/poetryarchive/singlePoem.do?poemId=5679

Extra Time

Ask students to imagine that they are either the maiden or the prince in Liz Lochhead's poem – writing updates on their social networking page as their feelings develop throughout the poem.

Lesson focus

Why are we teaching this?

In this lesson, students will learn about the conventions of courtly love and respond to the presentation of courtly love in poetry. This work provides an effective introduction to the concept of writing about literary context, which is required at GCSE level.

What are students learning?

Students will be able to:

● compare texts written in the same literary tradition.

How you could teach this

A variety of activities and approaches are provided on the right for you to select from and adapt to meet the needs of your students. The Kerboodle lesson player sequence is derived from these suggestions, to act as a starting point for your lesson.

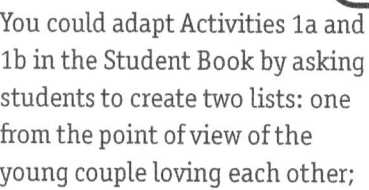

Teaching suggestions

Ignition

Loving adjectives

You could adapt Activities 1a and 1b in the Student Book by asking students to create two lists: one from the point of view of the young couple loving each other; the other where they dislike each other.

Resources
Student Book 3: Activities 1a and 1b, page 50

Optical illusions

Use the weblinks below to show students a range of optical illusions. Then ask them to discuss in small groups what they can see. Guide them to explore the idea that different people can see the same thing in different ways.

Resources
Weblinks: http://illusions.org/

http://www.echalk.co.uk/amusements/OpticalIllusions/illusions.html

http://kids.niehs.nih.gov/games/illusions/index.htm

Human chain

Display the question: 'Can you ignore a loved one's faults and love them anyway?' Ask students to position themselves along a continuum line, according to how much they think they could ignore a loved one's faults. Ask several students located in different places along the continuum line to explain their position.

Exploration

'Fidessa'

Ask students to read the extract from 'Fidessa' on page 51 of the Student Book (Sonnet 39) and consider the poet's view of the woman described. If required, the worksheet on Kerboodle will provide support for students in interpreting the poem and using evidence to explain a point of view.

Resources
Student Book 3: Activity 2, page 50

Kerboodle: 2.9 'Fidessa' by Bartholomew Griffin

Accurate descriptions?

Encourage students to think about the poet's descriptions of the woman in the poem – considering whether the presentation of the woman is realistic or not.

Resources
Student Book 3: Activity 3, page 50

and guidance

Courtly love

Show 'The stages of courtly love' presentation on Kerboodle and then follow up Activity 4 in the Student Book by asking students to consider the different stages of courtly love and write a modern version.

Resources

Student Book 3: Activity 4, page 51

Kerboodle: 2.9 The stages of courtly love

'To His Coy Mistress'

Encourage students to read Andrew Marvell's poem 'To His Coy Mistress' (supplied as a worksheet on Kerboodle) and discuss whether they think this is a love poem or something else. Ask them to find evidence in the text to support their point of view.

Resources

Kerboodle: 2.9 'To His Coy Mistress' by Andrew Marvell

Exploring the sonnet

Use the 'Exploring the sonnet' worksheet on Kerboodle to examine the sonnet convention. This worksheet contains two additional examples of Shakespeare's sonnets – 18 and 116 – for students to study.

Resources

Kerboodle: 2.9 Exploring the sonnet

Love me, love my poem!

Encourage students to write a poem in the style of courtly love. If required, suggest that they use the 'Writing a love poem' worksheet on Kerboodle to help them.

Resources

Kerboodle: 2.9 Writing a love poem

Explaining 'Sonnet 130'

Support Activity 5 in the Student Book by using the worksheet on Kerboodle to provide students with sentence starters and ideas to explain what Shakespeare was trying to achieve.

Resources

Student Book 3: Activity 5, page 52

Kerboodle: 2.9 Explaining 'Sonnet 130'

Comparing sonnets

The 'Comparing sonnets' worksheet on Kerboodle provides a comparison grid for students to complete in response to Activity 6 in the Student Book.

Resources

Student Book 3: Activity 6, page 53

Kerboodle: 2.9 Comparing sonnets

Consolidation

Sticky note plenary

Ask students to write down the three aspects of courtly love which most appeal to them – and explain why.

Phone a friend

Invite students to write down three questions they would like to ask as a result of this lesson, and choose other people to answer. Ensure that the focus is on the learning!

Mind-map

Allow students time to create a mind-map about the poetic genre that they have learned about in this lesson. Ask them to consider words and images carefully to support their ideas.

Extra Time

Ask students to write a diary entry by the author of 'Fidessa', in which he portrays her in a more realistic light.

Assessment focus

Why are we assessing this?

Students' creative writing is assessed at GCSE level. This lesson is an interesting and engaging way of introducing them to the formal assessment of creative writing, as well as assessing their understanding of the work carried out in this unit through the content and style of their writing.

What are students demonstrating?

Students will be able to:

- write a poem about family, friends or enemies.

How to deliver the assessment

Suggestions and guidance on how to set up and prepare your students for the assessment are provided, as well as possible approaches to marking the assessment.

Ignite English interview

You might like to play Ignite Interview Film 2 to the class, in which Nick Cope discusses writing and editing.

Resources
Kerboodle: 2 Ignite Interview Nick Cope Film 2 🎞

Alternative/additional assessment

There is an alternative end-of-unit assessment available on Kerboodle. This reading assessment can be used either in addition to or instead of the Student Book end-of-unit assessment.

Resources
Kerboodle: 2.10 Alternative end-of-unit assessment 📄

Assessment suggestions and guidance

Understanding the assessment

Check that students understand the assessment task and have read the instructions carefully. Emphasize that they are being assessed on their *writing* skills. Remind students to edit and proofread their work.

Resources
Student Book 3: pages 54–55

Planning

Students should begin by brainstorming the different conventions of poetry, and different attitudes to relationships, before making decisions about which relationship and which style they are going to use for their assessment. When they have made those decisions, they should make a note of key words that they want to use – using a dictionary and thesaurus to improve the quality of their writing.

Timing and writing expectation

Give students one hour (ideally one lesson) and expect between one half and two sides of A4, depending on the ability of the student.

Marking

You will want to mark this in line with departmental and school marking guidelines. If you wish, you could use the Ignite English marking scales provided on Kerboodle. Using the Ignite English marking scales will help you to identify specific strengths and areas for improvement in an individual student's writing. This may help you to set development targets as well as build a profile of your class as writers.

Refer to the KS3 National Curriculum and Ignite English mapping grids on pages 154–156 of this Teacher Companion to identify other Ignite English units where these writing skills are covered, or ask students to use the SPAG interactives on Kerboodle to address any areas identified for improvement. The Grammar Reference Guide on Kerboodle contains definitions and additional examples of each of the spelling, punctuation and grammar points covered in the interactives, for your reference.

Resources
Kerboodle: 2 Ignite English marking scales 📄

Kerboodle: SPAG interactives 🖱

Kerboodle: Grammar Reference Guide

Key for Kerboodle LRA resources   📄 Worksheet   🖱 Interactive activity   🎞 Video

Student Book answers

Below are the answers to any largely non-subjective Student Book activities contained within this unit.

Lesson 1

2 The poet and his mother are in his new house, measuring things. She is holding the 'zero end' (the bit of the tape measure which pulls out) and writing down the numbers that he calls out.

3 He and his mother are linked together by the tape, but also by their relationship and shared history. She is both his anchor, holding him down, and his kite, setting him free.

Lesson 2

1 Her pregnancy. The child is not yet born.

3 Round, white, featureless.

Lesson 4

2a That he will always be there for his friend, no matter what.

Lesson 5

3 The spelling of words like 'diwisions' and non-standard forms such as 'you and me is'. He also uses 'ain't' and 'anywheres'.

5 He has been 'finding fault' with Joe and judging him negatively, because he doesn't fit in in London. He thinks that he is better than Joe but comes to realise that he is wrong.

Lesson 6

1a The poet, Fleur Adcock, is the narrator. She is talking to her friend, Meg, who has died.

Lesson 8

1 The key ingredients of a traditional fairy tale are:
   - Prince
   - Princess
   - Wicked stepmother
   - Witch
   - Magic
   - Evil

2 Rapunzel and Rumplestiltskin

3 The maiden does not want to be rescued – she is happy where she is. The prince is not a hero – he is a rather pathetic character.

Lesson 9

2 That she is the most beautiful and amazing woman that he has ever seen or heard.

Unit 3: Exploring Difference

Unit overview

Why are we teaching this?

This unit is designed to develop students' skills in reading, writing and spoken English, by strengthening their understanding of the ways in which writers address the themes of **difference and conformity**. It offers them opportunities to respond to powerful texts that **challenge accepted notions of normality.** These themes often have a strong resonance with Year 9 students, as they develop a more-complex understanding of the demands of the society in which they live – the ways in which difference can be both tolerated and celebrated, but also the **pressures placed on individuals to conform.**

This unit contains a **wide range of fiction and non-fiction**, including extracts from classic texts from the English literary heritage, such as *Silas Marner* by George Eliot and William Golding's *Lord of the Flies*, alongside poetry, short stories, autobiography, newspaper articles, letters, and blog posts. The activities develop students' **critical-reading skills**. A variety of writing tasks are also included, allowing students to apply their knowledge of the **grammatical techniques** and **structural approaches** explored to their own writing in a range of forms.

What are the learning aims?

By the end of the unit, students will be able to:

- understand how writers develop complex themes within texts
- evaluate the ways in which writers use language to present meaning and manipulate their readers' responses
- study setting and characterization and analyse the effects of these in relation to theme
- analyse and make critical comparisons across texts which deal with similar themes, recognizing a range of poetic conventions and understanding how they have been used
- write a well-structured formal expository essay and other non-narrative texts, including personal letters and blog posts.

How will this be assessed?

Key assessment task	Focus for assessment
Student Book: Writing an expository essay in response to a reading question analysing the characterization of Ralph and Piggy in an extract from *Lord of The Flies* by William Golding.	<ul><li>Understanding the ways in which characterization contributes to the development of theme</li><li>Commenting on how language is used to convey meaning</li><li>Analysing the way in which the text is structured</li></ul>
Kerboodle: Presenting a short segment of a scripted radio programme on the theme of 'Exploring Difference'.	<ul><li>Using Standard English confidently, presenting ideas coherently and in a lively manner.</li><li>Demonstrating creativity in the selection of material and its presentation.</li><li>Presenting a range of views with sensitivity and engagement.</li></ul>

The end-of-unit assessment on Kerboodle can be used either instead of or in addition to the Student Book end-of-unit assessment.

Note that short Progress Checks also feature in this unit, providing formative assessment opportunities to support the students' learning.

Lesson sequence   This is a suggested lesson sequence, but you might choose to alter or add to it to suit your particular teaching needs.

Introducing the unit

1   Challenging Perceptions

- Share existing knowledge to discuss how society treats people who are seen to be different, and also reflect on their portrayal in various media.
- Respond to the Ignite Interview, featuring Nikki Emerson.
- Consider and discuss how works of art can challenge perceptions.
- Give a presentation expressing a viewpoint.

2 A Different Child	**3 Free at Last**	**4 Pushing the Limits**
• Identify the techniques used by a writer to convey thoughts and emotions. • Analyse a personal letter written for publication which describes personal experiences of difference. • Write a personal letter using figurative language to express emotion.	• Analyse structure by exploring the techniques used to build a sense of tension. • Explore characterization and experiment with this in your own writing. • Read and analyse an extract from *My Left Foot* by Christy Brown. • Write and perform a short monologue.	• Evaluate an author's purpose and experiment with extended metaphor. • Read and analyse a blog post by Wendy Booker. • Write a blog post about overcoming a personal challenge.
5 Making Your Mark	**6 Standing Out**	**7 The Outsider**
• Analyse characterization in a first-person narrative. • Read and analyse an extract from *The Somebody* by Danny Santiago, with an emphasis on characterization. • Write the next paragraph of the short story, creating an effective narrative voice.	• Explore how the theme of conformity is presented in two poems. • Read and discuss the poems 'For Heidi With Blue Hair' by Fleur Adcock and 'Warning' by Jenny Joseph. • Prepare a presentation about the selected poem.	• Explore characterization in a pre-1914 literary heritage novel. • Read and analyse an extract from *Silas Marner* by George Eliot.

8   Assessment

- Student Book: Read and analyse an extract from *Lord of the Flies* by William Golding.
- Kerboodle: Present a short segment of a scripted radio programme on the theme of 'Exploring Difference'.

Preparing to teach

Refresh your knowledge

You might find it helpful to refer to the following key points when planning your teaching of this unit.

- Difference, and the ways in which society regards it, is a common theme in both adult and children's literature. It can be found in almost every genre, from historical fiction (such as *Private Peaceful* and *The Boy in the Striped Pyjamas*), through fantasy books (such as the Harry Potter series), to humorous titles (such as *Bill's New Frock* by Anne Fine and *Cosmic* by Frank Cottrell Boyce). Reflect on those books your students have already read in the classroom that explore the themes of difference and conformity. Activating students' prior knowledge of relevant texts that they have already read will help them to engage with the new texts addressed by this unit.

- Non-fiction texts also offer a rich resource when exploring the theme of difference. From autobiographies and memoirs giving the reader insights into lives remote from their own, to letters and blogs where individuals can share their personal experiences of being different, non-fiction provides real-life examples for students to engage with. As you plan this unit, be on the lookout for contemporary news stories that help to illuminate the subject matter and themes of the texts addressed within this unit.

- Some of the stimuli texts included in this unit depict individuals with the conditions of autism, multiple sclerosis, cerebral palsy, and congenital disorders. It is important that the subject matter of these texts is handled sensitively in the classroom context. Emphasize that the ways in which these conditions are described in the texts are reflective of only those individuals concerned – and not necessarily every individual with that condition.

Links and further reading

- Quotes about 'conformity' and 'being different', to stimulate debate, can be found on: http://www.goodreads.com/quotes/tag/conformity http://www.brainyquote.com/quotes/keywords/being_different.html

- Recommendations for students' independent reading: *The Woman in White* by Wilkie Collins; *Private Peaceful* by Michael Morpurgo; *The Boy in the Striped Pyjamas* by John Boyne; *Freak the Mighty* by Rodman Philbrick; *To Kill a Mockingbird* by Harper Lee; *Fahrenheit 451* by Ray Bradbury; *Wonder* by R.J. Palacio; *Bill's New Frock* by Anne Fine; *Cosmic* by Frank Cottrell Boyce.

Please note that OUP is not responsible for third-party content. Although all links were correct at the time of publication, the content and location of this material may change.

Planning guidance and teaching tips

Think about how you can make the materials relevant to your students and responsive to their needs. Some suggested approaches to address key areas are provided below.

- Be prepared to work with students with **lower reading ages**, and **EAL** students, in one-to-one and guided group contexts, to support their reading of the texts included in this unit.

- Give students space to talk about and reflect on their reading. Creating purposeful opportunities for students to discuss and share ideas about a text, can help to engage those **more-reluctant readers** with negative attitudes towards reading.

- Use the **Ignite Interview** with Nikki Emerson in the Student Book, or play the Ignite Interview films on Kerboodle, to reinforce students' awareness of the theme.

- **Modelling** responses to reading for students would be particularly beneficial for students in this unit. Developing students' skills in the elements they need to construct an expository essay will help to prepare them for the end-of-unit assessment.

- Refer to the **Grammar Reference Guide** on Kerboodle for definitions and exemplars of the specific grammar and punctuation terms covered in this unit, as highlighted by the Literacy Feature icon. Kerboodle also provides **SPAG interactives** to help improve the technical accuracy of students' writing and the application of grammar in context. You can assign specific SPAG interactives to individual students, or groups of students, according to their needs.

- Students often struggle when attempting to **trace themes** in a text, because they are expressed through the orchestration of every aspect of the writing: narrative, character, setting, and language. Over the course of this unit, students will be given the opportunity to explore each of these aspects separately, with the aim of bringing them all together in the assessment task. This will provide excellent preparation for their GCSE studies, especially if they are going to study texts such as *Lord of the Flies*, *To Kill a Mockingbird* and *Of Mice and Men* – all of which explore the theme of difference to some extent.

Lesson focus

Why are we teaching this?

This lesson launches the unit by introducing the theme of difference and allowing students to use their prior knowledge to discuss how society treats people who are seen to be different. They also have the opportunity to consider ways in which works of art can challenge perceptions and assumptions, by studying a newspaper article about Marc Quinn's famous sculpture of Alison Lapper in Trafalgar Square.

What are students learning?

Students will be able to:

- consider and discuss how works of art can challenge perceptions
- give a presentation expressing a viewpoint.

How you could teach this

A variety of activities and approaches are provided on the right for you to select from and adapt to meet the needs of your students. The Kerboodle lesson player sequence is derived from these suggestions, to act as a starting point for your lesson.

Answers

Answers to Student Book activities, where relevant, can be found on page 81.

Teaching suggestions

Ignition

Ignite English interview

You might like to play Ignite Interview Film 1 to the class. In this film we are introduced to Nikki Emerson, wheelchair track athlete, and her thoughts about difference.

Resources

Kerboodle: 3 Ignite Interview Nikki Emerson Film 1

Are we tolerant?

Ask students to vote on whether they think we are a tolerant or intolerant society. As a class, discuss how society treats people who are seen to be different. End the discussion by voting again and see if any students have changed their views.

Resources

Student Book 3: Activity 1, page 57

Wider reading

Ask students to suggest books, films and TV programmes that deal with the theme of difference, e.g. *Wonder*. Discuss the appeal of these sources and how they help readers and viewers to begin to understand what it is like to be different – or seen as different.

Resources

Student Book 3: Activity 2, page 57

Exploration

The power of an image

Use the 'Challenging perceptions' image gallery on Kerboodle to show students a photograph of the statue of Alison Lapper pregnant on the fourth plinth in Trafalgar Square, before asking them to jot down their thoughts and feelings on sticky notes. When they have done this, select some of their responses (anonymously) for class discussion. Then show the image of the Venus de Milo and discuss any perceived similarities and differences with Alison Lapper's statue. Finally, show the image of the 2012 Paralympics Opening Ceremony and discuss its meaning and relevance.

Resources

Student Book 3: Activity 1, page 58

Kerboodle: 3.1 Challenging perceptions

What do you think?

As a formal response to Activity 1 in the Student Book, discuss students' views about the Alison Lapper statue and its exhibition, either as a class or in small groups. Model how to build on what others say by taking an active role in the discussion.

Resources

Student Book 3: Activity 1, page 58

 Lesson Player Image Video Worksheet

and guidance

Consolidation

Alison Lapper

Use the weblink below to allow students to read the *Mirror* newspaper article about Alison Lapper's relationship with her teenage son, and then discuss her views about society's treatment of disabled people.

Resources

Weblink: http://www.mirror.co.uk/news/real-life-stories/alison-lapper-happy-son-parys-1734221

Making a presentation

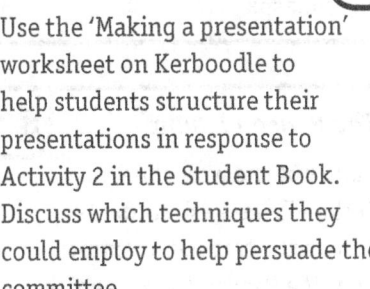

Use the 'Making a presentation' worksheet on Kerboodle to help students structure their presentations in response to Activity 2 in the Student Book. Discuss which techniques they could employ to help persuade the committee.

Resources

Student Book 3: Activity 2, page 58

Kerboodle: 3.1 Making a presentation

Creative writing

Use the photograph of the Alison Lapper statue in Trafalgar Square (from the 'Challenging perceptions' image gallery on Kerboodle) as inspiration for students' creative writing. Ask them to write a short story in which a mother or father is walking across Trafalgar Square with their young child. The child insists on stopping in front of the statue and begins to ask questions. How will the parent answer? Will he or she try to get the child to move on?

Documentary

Use the weblink below to show students a *Guardian* article containing an extract from Alison Lapper's autobiography, *My Life In My Hands*. Discuss how the scene where Alison meets her birth mother could be filmed in a dramatization of her life. Ask students to create a storyboard for this scene, focusing on the paragraph beginning 'The day we met was a day like any other …'.

Resources

Weblink: http://www.theguardian.com/artanddesign/2005/sep/03/art1

Alternative views

Show students the 'Alternative views' presentation on Kerboodle, which presents two different people's responses to the statue of Alison Lapper. Ask students to discuss these views and comment on whether they agree or disagree with each of them – and why.

Resources

Kerboodle: 3.1 Alternative views

Reconsidering personal views

Ask students to look again at the thoughts they jotted down on sticky notes at the beginning of the lesson. Encourage them to reflect on whether they would add or change anything now.

Evaluation

Two stars and a wish: ask students to decide on two things they did well in their presentation and one thing they could improve.

Extra Time

Ask students to find out more about Alison Lapper.

⚲ Weblink   🖥 Presentation   🔲 Interactive activity

Lesson focus

Why are we teaching this?

This lesson focuses on a personal letter from a mother to her autistic son – written for a public audience. The complex thoughts and feelings expressed in the letter, which is written with great care and technical skill, provide an appropriate challenge for students' reading – allowing them to analyse how the writer structures the letter and uses figurative language to express her emotional journey effectively.

What are students learning?

Students will be able to:

- identify the techniques used by a writer to convey thoughts and emotions.

How you could teach this

A variety of activities and approaches are provided on the right for you to select from and adapt to meet the needs of your students. The Kerboodle lesson player sequence is derived from these suggestions, to act as a starting point for your lesson.

Answers

Answers to Student Book activities, where relevant, can be found on page 81.

Teaching suggestions

Ignition

Letter to anyone

Pose the following question to the class: 'If you could write a letter to anyone, alive or dead, who would it be and what would you say?' Discuss students' responses and share your own views.

A letter to …

Explain the format of *The Guardian's* 'A Letter to …' feature, e.g. the letter is anonymous and is never sent. Ask students to think about why a writer might find this structure helpful when tackling difficult or emotional subject matter.

Words and judgements

Using the 'Words and judgements' interactive activity on Kerboodle, ask students to discuss the descriptions and their connotations before categorizing them as positive or negative.

Resources

Kerboodle: 3.2 Words and judgements

Exploration

Understanding autism

Ask students what they already know about autism. This subject needs to be handled sensitively, because the class may include students who have the condition, or who have autistic relatives or friends. Use information from the weblink below to build or reinforce students' understanding of the condition.

Resources

Weblink: http://www.autism.org.uk/about-autism/autism-and-asperger-syndrome-an-introduction/what-is-autism.aspx

The Reason I Jump

Hand out the worksheet on Kerboodle and ask students to read the translated extract from *The Reason I Jump*, which was written by a 13-year-old Japanese schoolboy with autism (called Naoki Higashida). Discuss how this extract might help students to understand more about autism. The extract was originally quoted in the following weblink article, which may also provide some useful background information about this condition for discussion.

Resources

Kerboodle: 3.2 *The Reason I Jump* extract

Weblink: http://www.guardian.co.uk/society/2013/jun/29/david-mitchell-my-sons-autism

and guidance

Consolidation

Reasons for writing

In response to Activity 1 in the Student Book, ask students to suggest possible reasons why the mother chose to write this letter. Vote on which reason they think is the best. Also discuss the letter's audience, and how the author might want her writing to affect her readers.

Resources

Student Book 3: Activity 1, page 60

Figurative language

Use the 'Figurative language' worksheet on Kerboodle to support lower-achieving students with Activity 2 in the Student Book.

Resources

Student Book 3: Activity 2, page 60

Kerboodle: 3.2 Figurative language

Word list

Support lower-achieving students with Activity 3a in the Student Book by providing them with the following word list to choose from: wonder, confusion, acceptance, love, hurt, admiration, worry, pride, concern, relief, grief, humour, delight, protectiveness.

Resources

Student Book 3: Activity 3a, page 61

Modelling writing

Before students attempt Activity 4 in the Student Book, model writing the opening of a personal letter – using figurative language to express your emotions. To avoid any potential sensitivity around this activity, you could write in role as a character from a novel students have read in class, and then ask students to do the same.

Resources

Student Book 3: Activity 4, page 61

Finding figurative language

Ask students to re-read the mother's letter and choose other examples of figurative language (they should also look for metaphors and similes). Then ask them to explain what makes their chosen examples effective. You could feed back as a class and compare students' choices and explanations.

Summarizing

Ask students, using no more than 30 words, to describe the emotional journey travelled by the mother. Take feedback and discuss the key points that students have summarized.

Progress Check

Building on Activity 4 in the Student Book, students should highlight the figurative language they used in their own letters and reflect on its effectiveness.

Resources

Student Book 3: Activity 4, page 61

Extra Time

Ask students to search online to find and read other 'A letter to ...' from *The Guardian* archive.

 Weblink   🖥 Presentation   🖰 Interactive activity

Lesson focus

Why are we teaching this?

This lesson allows students to explore characterization through their reading of an extract from Christy Brown's acclaimed autobiography, *My Left Foot*. In the extract included in the Student Book, the author describes a defining moment in his life. Students then explore the ways in which he uses language to create the tension of that moment.

What are students learning?

Students will be able to:

- analyse structure by exploring the techniques used to build a sense of tension
- explore characterization and experiment with this in their own writing.

How you could teach this

A variety of activities and approaches are provided on the right for you to select from and adapt to meet the needs of your students. The Kerboodle lesson player sequence is derived from these suggestions, to act as a starting point for your lesson.

Answers

Answers to Student Book activities, where relevant, can be found on page 81.

Teaching suggestions

Ignition

My Left Foot

Display the front cover of *My Left Foot* from Kerboodle and ask students to discuss what they think this book will be about. Elicit suggestions about the setting and subject matter of the book.

Resources
Kerboodle: 3.3 The front cover of *My Left Foot*

Stepping into another's shoes

Set students the task of drawing each other's portraits, using the 'wrong' hand. This will help them to understand what it feels like to not have full control of their motor functions. Discuss their thoughts and feelings about this experience.

Understanding cerebral palsy

Ask students what they already know about cerebral palsy. This subject will need to be handled sensitively, because the class may include students who have the condition, or who have relatives or friends affected by it. Use information from the weblink below to build or reinforce students' understanding of the condition.

Resources
Weblink: http://www.nhs.uk/conditions/Cerebral-palsy/Pages/Introduction.aspx

Exploration

Christy's character

You could support lower-achieving students with Activity 1 in the Student Book by supplying some vocabulary for them to choose from: *pathetic, proud, desperate, stupid, determined, fascinated, lonely, curious, frustrated, bored, sad, impulsive, loved, ignored.* Ask students to support their choices with evidence from the text.

Resources
Student Book 3: Activity 1, page 64

Selecting sentences

In response to Activity 2 in the Student Book, ask students to select three 'tense sentences' from the text: one sentence that describes tense actions; one sentence that describes the family's tense reactions; one sentence communicating Christy's thoughts and feelings. Discuss students' choices and choose one or two sentences to analyse.

Resources
Student Book 3: Activity 2, page 65

and guidance

Building tension

Use the 'Building tension' presentation on Kerboodle to support students' analyses in response to Activity 2 in the Student Book – focusing on sentence structure, punctuation and word choice.

Resources

Student Book 3: Activity 2, page 65

Kerboodle: 3.3 Building tension

Family feelings

Read through the extract again and stop at important moments (e.g. 'Nobody stirred' in paragraph five). Ask students to say or write what other members of the family might be thinking at these points in the narrative.

Christy's mother

Christy's mother is absent from the room during the first half of the extract. Ask students to discuss how she might have felt when she came into the room, as well as her possible feelings as she helped her son. Encourage students to draw on this discussion as they write and perform their monologues for Activity 3 in the Student Book. You could also distribute the 'Writing a monologue' worksheet from Kerboodle to help students, if required.

Resources

Student Book 3: Activity 3, page 65

Kerboodle: 3.3 Writing a monologue

A conversation

Ask students to imagine, perform and then write a conversation between Christy's mother and father after the events described in the passage.

The film

Explain that *My Left Foot* was made into an Oscar-winning film – famous for the way in which the actor Daniel Day-Lewis used method acting to prepare for the role. Use the first two weblinks below to show the class some stills from the film. Then discuss the ethics of an able-bodied actor playing a disabled part. You could also ask higher-achieving students to read and discuss *The Guardian* article on the same theme, which can be accessed through the third weblink below.

Resources

Weblinks:

http://tinyurl.com/pnt9y4l

http://tinyurl.com/ppqnzp2

http://www.guardian.co.uk/stage/theatreblog/2013/jun/20/why-acceptable-daniel-radcliffe-disabled-character

Consolidation

Independent analysis

Ask students to work independently to analyse the paragraph from *My Left Foot* in the Student Book that begins 'I held it tightly between my toes' (paragraph 5, page 66). Say that they should aim to explain how the sentence structures used help to build a sense of tension.

A sense of struggle

Explain that when Daniel Day-Lewis was filming *My Left Foot*, he never left his wheelchair and stayed in role at all times. Drawing on the techniques they have explored in the extract, ask students to write a short piece imagining what it might feel like to spend a day like Christy Brown. They should write in the first person and aim to convey a sense of the struggle through their choice of sentences and vocabulary.

Dramatic interpretation

Show the clip from the film version of *My Left Foot* that portrays the scene described in the Student Book extract. Discuss how effectively the scene in the film builds a sense of tension and the techniques it uses to do this.

Extra Time

Ask students to read *My Left Foot*, or other autobiographies by people who have overcome great challenges in their lives.

🔗 Weblink   💻 Presentation   🔲 Interactive activity

Lesson focus

Why are we teaching this?

This lesson allows students to explore how themes can be presented in non-fiction texts, and also to investigate how writers can use extended metaphors. By reading an extract from the mountaineer Wendy Booker's blog, students can see how she links her climbing with her struggle against multiple sclerosis. Considering the purpose and audience of this form of writing, students also have the opportunity to write their own blog entries – allowing them to build links with the writing they do outside school.

What are students learning?

Students will be able to:

- evaluate an author's purpose and experiment with extended metaphor.

How you could teach this

A variety of activities and approaches are provided on the right for you to select from and adapt to meet the needs of your students. The Kerboodle lesson player sequence is derived from these suggestions, to act as a starting point for your lesson.

> **Answers**
>
> Answers to Student Book activities, where relevant, can be found on page 81.

Teaching suggestions

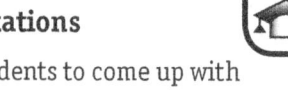

Ignition

Blogging

Discuss the idea of blogging as a class. Elicit suggestions for blogs students follow, or ones they write themselves. Ask them to consider the advantages and disadvantages of blogging, in comparison with traditional publishing.

Expectations

Ask students to come up with words and phrases to describe a mountaineer. Write them on the whiteboard and refer to them later in the lesson to see if the class think they apply to Wendy Booker.

Understanding multiple sclerosis

Ask students what they already know about multiple sclerosis. This subject needs to be handled sensitively, because the class may include students who have the condition, or who have relatives or friends affected by it. Use information from the weblink below to build or reinforce students' understanding of the condition.

Resources
Weblink: http://www.mssociety.org.uk/what-is-ms

Exploration

Purpose and audience

In response to Activity 1 in the Student Book, discuss with the class why Wendy Booker might have chosen to share the entry quoted on page 69 on her blog. Prompt students to activate their prior knowledge of blogging as they comment on the purpose of her writing and her potential audience.

Resources
Student Book 3: Activity 1, page 68

Extended metaphor

Display the poem 'Scaffolding' by Seamus Heaney on Kerboodle to further explore the use of extended metaphor. Discuss how Wendy Booker acts out her metaphor in her life.

Resources
Student Book 3: Activity 2, page 68

Kerboodle: 3.4 'Scaffolding' by Seamus Heaney

Tagging

In response to Activity 3 in the Student Book, use the 'Abstract nouns' worksheet on Kerboodle to support lower-achieving students with nouns they could use to describe the theme of the blog.

Resources
Student Book 3: Activity 3, page 68

Kerboodle: 3.4 Abstract nouns

and guidance

Consolidation

Mountain climbing

As a class, discuss the question: 'Is mountain climbing a sport?' Ask students to write a short summary of Booker's views about climbing, and then to use the Internet to research the activity further (the weblink below would be a useful start). Then ask them to use their research to create a poster designed to encourage more young people to take up mountain climbing.

Resources
Weblink: http://www. mountainclimbing.net/

Presentation

Ask students to use the three weblinks below to research Wendy Booker and prepare a short presentation about her and her achievements to inspire people who have been diagnosed with multiple sclerosis.

Resources
Weblinks:
http://www.wendybooker.net/

http://tinyurl.com/bnt23h5

http://climbing.about.com/ od/mountainclimbing/a/ BookerInterview.htm

Poetry

As a class, discuss how and why mountains have provided writers with powerful images. Ask students to read a range of poetry from the following weblink that describes mountains, or uses them as a metaphor.

Resources
Weblink: http://www. blackcatpoems.com/m/ mountain_poems.html

Ignite English interview

You might like to play Ignite Interview Film 2 to the class, in which Nikki Emerson discusses being an athlete.

Resources
Kerboodle: 3 Ignite Interview Nikki Emerson Film 2

Writing a blog

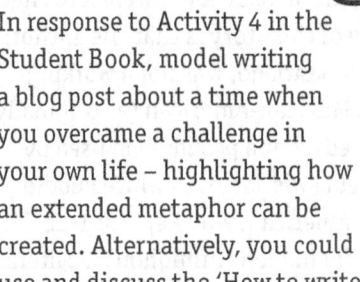

In response to Activity 4 in the Student Book, model writing a blog post about a time when you overcame a challenge in your own life – highlighting how an extended metaphor can be created. Alternatively, you could use and discuss the 'How to write a blog' worksheet on Kerboodle.

Resources
Student Book 3: Activity 4, page 68

Kerboodle: 3.4 How to write a blog

Progress Check

Ask students to assess each other's blog posts, as outlined in the Progress Check in the Student Book (page 69).

Blogging is …

Ask students to suggest the top three reasons for writing a blog. Discuss and vote on these as a class. Use the weblink below to show examples of reasons given by other teen bloggers.

Resources
Weblink: http://www.guardian. co.uk/technology/2009/sep/ 09/teenage-bloggers

Extra Time

Ask students to find and follow a blog about one of their interests.

Lesson focus

Why are we teaching this?

This lesson allows students to analyse characterization by exploring how an author constructs the character of the main protagonist in an extract from a short story entitled *The Somebody*. An additional layer of interest to the study of this story is that the author, Danny Santiago, was not a working-class Mexican-American (as originally claimed), but a pseudonym used by Daniel Lewis James (a white middle-class American, who kept his true identity hidden throughout his literary career).

What are students learning?

Students will be able to:
- analyse characterization in a first-person narrative.

How you could teach this

A variety of activities and approaches are provided on the right for you to select from and adapt to meet the needs of your students. The Kerboodle lesson player sequence is derived from these suggestions, to act as a starting point for your lesson.

Answers

Answers to Student Book activities, where relevant, can be found on page 81.

Teaching suggestions

Ignition

Graffiti

Use the 'Graffiti' image gallery on Kerboodle to show students some examples of graffiti – some of which are very artistic and well executed, and others merely 'tags'. Ask students to discuss their attitudes towards graffiti.

Resources
Kerboodle: 3.5 Graffiti

The Somebody

Before reading the extract in the Student Book, ask the class to discuss the title and possible theme of the story: What is a 'somebody'? What might the story be about? Elicit predictions from the class about the possible theme, and then discuss which of them students think are the most likely.

Setting

Use Google Street View, or other online mapping tools, to explore Clover Street, Los Angeles (the inspiration for Shamrock Street in the story, although there are no houses there now). Ask students what impressions they get of the neighbourhood.

Exploration

The title

After they have read the extract in the Student Book, give students a 50-word limit to explain why the author might have called his story *The Somebody*. Elicit responses and discuss the reasons given.

Resources
Student Book 3: Activity 1, page 70

Chato's character and voice

You could support lower-achieving students by using shared reading to read the Student Book extract and then discuss what impression it gives of Chato's character and voice. Alternatively, you could use the 'Annotated paragraph' worksheet on Kerboodle to provide some example comments about paragraph 4 of the Student Book extract, to stimulate students' own analysis of the rest of the extract.

Resources
Student Book 3: Activity 2, page 70

Kerboodle: 3.5 Annotated paragraph

and guidance

Chato's character

Use the 'Attitudes and opinions' worksheet on Kerboodle to prompt students' exploration of Chato's attitudes and opinions about the following: his gang, his father, his mother, violence, graffiti, school, babies, his neighbourhood.

Resources

Student Book 3: Activity 2, page 70

Kerboodle: 3.5 Attitudes and opinions

Character profile

You could ask students to use the 'Character profile' worksheet on Kerboodle to create a character profile for Chato.

Resources

Kerboodle: 3.5 Character profile

Other views

Discuss how other characters in the story might view Chato, e.g. his father, his mother, his gang. Ask students to role-play a conversation between one of these characters and Chato.

Consolidation

Creating your own character

Ask students to write the opening of a short story set in their own neighbourhood. Challenge them to write the story in the first person, using the voice of a boy or girl who is dissatisfied with their life.

The truth behind the story

Reveal Danny Santiago's true identity to the class. Discuss whether they feel that it invalidates Santiago's insights into Chicano culture. Use the weblink below to provide further information.

Resources

Weblink: http://en.wikipedia. org/wiki/Daniel_Lewis_James

Progress Check

You could ask students to use the 'Annotated paragraph' worksheet on Kerboodle to support a peer-assessment of their partner's paragraphs from the Extra Time activity.

Resources

Kerboodle: 3.5 Annotated paragraph

Extra Time

Ask students to write the next few paragraphs of the story from the Student Book. Encourage them to think about how they could show more about Chato's character.

Lesson focus

Why are we teaching this?

In this lesson, students read and explore two poems dealing with the desire to be different by individuals who challenge conformity. The comparison of these two poems also gives students the opportunity to start developing the analytical skills needed for GCSE studies.

What are students learning?

Students will be able to:

- explore how the theme of conformity is presented in two poems.

How you could teach this

A variety of activities and approaches are provided on the right for you to select from and adapt to meet the needs of your students. The Kerboodle lesson player sequence is derived from these suggestions, to act as a starting point for your lesson.

Answers

Answers to Student Book activities, where relevant, can be found on page 81.

Teaching suggestions

Ignition

What is an anthology?

Check that students understand what an anthology is. Using examples from your bookshelves, or the school library, discuss the nature of poetry anthologies with the class. Ask them to consider how editors choose poems for inclusion and what makes a good anthology. You could use the 'Anthology evaluation' worksheet on Kerboodle to support this task.

Resources

Kerboodle: 3.6 Anthology evaluation

School uniform

Display your school's dress code rules. Discuss which rules students have challenged – or would like to challenge – and their reasons why.

Being different

Discuss why some people choose to be different. Using the 'Conformity' interactive activity on Kerboodle, ask students to consider what 'conformity' means. Ask the class to name any teenage sub-cultures they are aware of, such as 'goths' and 'emos'. You could use the 'Alternative images' image gallery on Kerboodle to prompt discussion about the appeal of these and other sub-cultures.

Resources

Kerboodle: 3.6 Alternative images

Kerboodle: 3.6 Conformity

Exploration

Reading the poems

Assign the reading of the two poems on page 75 of the Student Book to different groups of students, to ensure that both poems are read. As they read, encourage students to consider the meaning of the poem and the questions they wish to ask. Elicit some of these questions and discuss them as a class.

Resources

Student Book 3: Activity 1, page 74

Discussing the poems

Before they begin Activity 2 in the Student Book, you could give lower-achieving students copies of the 'Analysis support' worksheet on Kerboodle, to support their discussion of the two poems.

Resources

Student Book 3: Activity 2, page 74

Kerboodle: 3.6 Analysis support

Role-play

Use each poem in the Student Book as the stimulus for a role-play exploring reactions to the way the character behaves. Students studying 'For Heidi With Blue Hair' could role-play the conversation with the Head Teacher, whilst students studying 'Warning' could explore how the poet's children or grandchildren might react.

and guidance

Consolidation

Comparing the poems

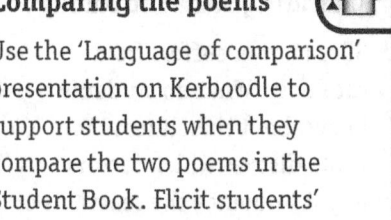

Use the 'Language of comparison' presentation on Kerboodle to support students when they compare the two poems in the Student Book. Elicit students' responses and collate the most-effective points on the board. Highlight how the various points could be grouped into paragraphs to create a coherent comparative response.

Resources

Kerboodle: 3.6 Language of comparison

Newspaper report

Ask students to read the newspaper report on the weblink below about a girl with dyed-red hair being sent home from school. Then ask them to use 'For Heidi With Blue Hair' as the basis for a similar local newspaper article.

Resources

Weblink: http://www.manchestereveningnews.co.uk/news/greater-manchester-news/seeing-red-girl-sent-home-695641

Performing poetry

Use Internet search engines to find a video of Jenny Joseph reading her poem 'Warning'. Discuss whether the poet's reading of her poem reflected the way students heard it in their mind.

The Red Hat Society

Use the two weblinks below to discuss and explore how the poem 'Warning' inspired the formation of a movement to encourage women to see old age positively.

Resources

Weblinks:
http://www.redhatsociety.com/

http://britishredhatters2.weebly.com/index.html

Creative writing

Ask students to write their own poem about the desire to be different. Encourage them to use some of the poetic conventions they have explored in their reading of 'For Heidi With Blue Hair' and 'Warning'.

Blurbs

Ask students to write a blurb for the back cover of the *Challenging Conformity* anthology. Look at examples of blurbs from other poetry anthologies and discuss what makes a good blurb.

Presentation evaluation

In response to Activity 3 in the Student Book, invite the school librarian to listen to the presentations in role as the editor of the *Challenging Conformity* anthology.

Resources

Student Book 3: Activity 3, page 74

Imagery

Encourage students to select images to accompany the reading of their chosen poem.

Extra Time

Ask students to find and read other poems that deal with the theme of challenging conformity.

Lesson focus

Why are we teaching this?

In this lesson, students will use an extract from a literary heritage novel to explore the portrayal of an outsider. Silas Marner, as well as being a geographic outsider, also suffers from catalepsy, so we – the reader – can see the ways in which the villagers react to both.

What are students learning?

Students will be able to:

- analyse characterization in a pre-1914 novel from the literary heritage.

How you could teach this

A variety of activities and approaches are provided on the right for you to select from and adapt to meet the needs of your students. The Kerboodle lesson player sequence is derived from these suggestions, to act as a starting point for your lesson.

Answers

Answers to Student Book activities, where relevant, can be found on page 81.

Teaching suggestions

Ignition

Exploring the context

Activate students' prior knowledge of early 19th-century England, particularly rural England. Collate the terms they use on the whiteboard (to refer to again once they have had the chance to read the extract from *Silas Marner* on page 77 of the Student Book). You could use the weblink below to stimulate discussion further.

Resources
Weblink: http://www.bbc.co.uk/history/british/victorians/exodus_01.shtml

Silas Marner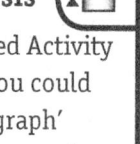

Display a range of images of the characters and setting of *Silas Marner*, as portrayed on the covers of different editions of the novel (or from television or film portrayals). An Internet search will produce many useful examples to prompt class discussion. Do the images match student first impressions on reading the extract?

The outsider

Pose the question: 'Why can there be a negative reaction to an outsider?' Elicit responses and discuss students' views about the pressures that an outsider might have faced in either today's society or when George Eliot was writing.

Exploration

Changing social attitudes

Silas Marner suffers from catalepsy. What do students know about this illness? You could discuss which factors might influence the reactions of the 19th-century villagers to his illness. How might social attitudes to an illness like this differ now compared to when the novel was written and set?

Resources
Student Book 3: Activity 2, page 76

Close character analysis

After they have completed Activity 3 in the Student Book, you could use the 'Annotated paragraph' worksheet on Kerboodle to explore in detail with students how George Eliot presents Silas Marner and the villagers in this extract.

Resources
Student Book 3: Activity 3, page 76

Kerboodle: 3.7 Annotated paragraph

From page to screen

Ask students to use the extract on page 77 of the Student Book as the basis for a film storyboard. Encourage them to consider the camera shots that could be used, as well as the sound effects and music.

and guidance

Consolidation

George Eliot

Discuss with the class what they already know about George Eliot. For instance, do they know that she was a woman and that her real name was Mary Ann Evans? Ask why a female writer at that time would use a male penname. You could use the weblink below to stimulate discussion further.

Resources
Weblink:
http://www3.shropshire-cc.gov.uk/eliotg.htm

Vocabulary

Challenge students to replace some of the archaic and ornate vocabulary in the Student Book extract with simpler modern equivalents. Discuss how this might change the sense and tone of the writing. (You may want to make thesauruses available to support this activity.)

A modern meeting

Ask students to describe a similar scene in a modern-day setting. You could provide them with the following ideas as stimuli for their writing:

- A new student joins your class from another part of the country.
- Someone new moves into your street or village. They are new to the area.

Description

Ask students to write their own description of an outsider. Encourage them to include long, complex sentences and punctuation to develop descriptive detail.

Evaluation

Two stars and a wish: If students completed the Extra Time activity, ask them to identify two things they did well in their writing and one thing that they could improve.

Preferences

As modern readers, ask students to discuss their views about George Eliot's writing style. Encourage them to compare it with the style of those writers whose works they read for pleasure, and to discuss the strengths and weaknesses of the different writing styles.

Extra Time

Ask students what life was like in the village of Raveloe for Silas Marner. Ask them to write two or three paragraphs from his perspective, based on what they have learned from the Student Book extract. You could also show them another passage from the novel to enhance their understanding.

Weblink   Presentation   Interactive activity

Assessment focus

Why are we assessing this?

This unit has developed students' critical-reading skills. They have read a range of extracts from fiction and non-fiction, considering how language (including figurative language, vocabulary choice, grammar and text structure) is used to present meaning, and studying characterization and setting to explore how they reflect the themes of the text. This assessment now enables students to bring these skills together as they write an expository essay in response to a reading question on the characterization in an extract from *Lord of the Flies* by William Golding.

What are students demonstrating?

Students will be able to comment on:

- the characterization of Ralph and Piggy in the extract
- how language is used to convey meaning
- the way the extract is structured.

How to deliver the assessment

Suggestions and guidance on how to set up and prepare your students for the assessment are provided, as well as possible approaches to marking the assessment.

Alternative/additional assessment

There is an alternative end-of-unit assessment available on Kerboodle. This assessment leads to a spoken English outcome and can be used either in addition to or instead of the Student Book end-of-unit assessment.

Resources
Kerboodle: 3.8 Alternative end-of-unit assessment 🖹

Assessment suggestions and guidance

Understanding the assessment

Check that students understand the assessment task set. Emphasize that they are being tested on their reading skills, and that they should draw on the skills developed throughout this unit.

Resources
Student Book 3: pages 78–81

Planning

Remind students that they will need to plan their expository essay, thinking about the points they want to make to answer the question and the best way to organize them.

Completing the assessment

Remind students to refer to evidence and quotations from the text, and to edit their first draft and proofread their work.

Timing and writing expectation

Give students one hour (ideally one lesson) and expect approximately two to three A4 pages.

Marking

You will want to mark this in line with departmental and school marking guidelines. If you wish, you could use the Ignite English marking scales provided on Kerboodle. Using the Ignite English marking scales will help you to identify specific strengths and areas for improvement in an individual student's critical-reading skills. This may help you to set development targets as well as build a profile of your class as critical readers.

Refer to the KS3 National Curriculum and Ignite English mapping grids on pages 154–156 of this Teacher Companion to identify other Ignite English units where these reading skills are covered, or ask students to use the SPAG interactives on Kerboodle to address any areas identified for improvement. The Grammar Reference Guide on Kerboodle contains definitions and additional examples of each of the spelling, punctuation and grammar points covered in the interactives, for your reference.

Resources
Kerboodle: 3 Ignite English marking scales 🖹

Kerboodle: SPAG interactives 🖰

Kerboodle: Grammar Reference Guide

Key for Kerboodle LRA resources   🖹 Worksheet   🖰 Interactive activity

Student Book answers

The activities in this particular Student Book unit are quite subjective, so no answers have been provided for this section. However, several of the digital resources on Kerboodle do provide annotated source material for use during student feedback.

Unit 4: My Life, My Choices
Unit overview

Why are we teaching this?

This unit considers a range of **non-fiction texts**, which together enable students to explore the kinds of choices that young people have to make in their everyday lives. Engaging Year 9 students can be challenging, so it aims to **capitalize on their interests and pursuits** outside of school. Students of this age are starting to define themselves through their **choices** of social activities, fashion and music. They are also accelerating their journeys towards **independence** and making **responsible decisions** about their futures.

The theme of choice runs throughout the unit, with each lesson looking at how writers have addressed this question in different ways. As students consider the overall ideas, they will also look at the techniques and forms that writers use to create different effects on the reader.

What are the learning aims?

By the end of the unit, students will be able to:
- discuss a range of approaches to conveying a message or idea
- comment on the effect of writers' language choices and grammatical features
- analyse how texts are structured and explore how form contributes to meaning
- develop personal and critical responses
- appreciate different viewpoints, angles and attitudes in non-fiction texts
- understand fact and opinion.

How will this be assessed?

Key assessment task	Focus for assessment
Student Book: Writing a feature article for a new website aimed at teenagers, about a topic that young people would find interesting.	• Showing awareness of audience, purpose and tone. • Using structure and form effectively. • Using grammar and punctuation accurately. • Ensuring that writing is engaging and sustained.
Kerboodle: Giving a presentation advocating the inclusion of a particular person in a display about inspirational figures.	• Using Standard English to communicate ideas, selecting persuasive evidence and examples. • Speaking clearly and fluently, selecting an appropriate tone, pace and intonation. • Using non-verbal techniques and other methods to maintain an audience's interest. • Responding effectively to questions.

The end-of-unit assessment on Kerboodle can be used either instead of or in addition to the Student Book end-of-unit assessment.

Note that short Progress Checks also feature in this unit, providing formative assessment opportunities to support students' learning.

Lesson sequence

This is a suggested lesson sequence, but you might choose to alter or add to it to suit your particular teaching needs.

Introducing the unit

1 Have Your Say

- Record ideas for the contents of a new magazine for young people.
- Respond to the Ignite Interview featuring Lisa Sewards.
- Discuss an issue and prepare a presentation to convey a viewpoint.
- Examine extracts from non-fiction texts to generate ideas.
- Plan a persuasive presentation using rhetorical techniques.

---

2 Getting What You Want	**3 A Sporting Chance**	**4 Parental Pressure**
- Explore the use of persuasive devices in a campaign text. - Assess the structure and use of persuasive devices in an online petition. - Write an online petition to lobby for better youth facilities.	- Explore how writers present arguments and counter-arguments. - Examine the arguments put forward in two extracts about competitive and non-competitive sport. - Write a letter or email weighing up the pros and cons of competitive sports.	- Evaluate the effect of expert opinion and statistical information. - Explore emotive language. - Write a script for a scene in which a young person makes a stand.
5 Fashion Victims	**6 Cheapskates**	**7 Branding: Slavery or Loyalty?**
- Understand how writers use language to engage the reader. - Analyse vocabulary choices and language devices. - Write a short description of a fashion trend for an online magazine.	- Use talk and role-play to explore complex issues. - Explore angles and design questions. - Role-play interviews and use them to inform a draft article.	- Identify how writers convey their attitude to a subject. - Use context to explain the meanings of words. - Make links between openings and endings to create a complete argument.
8 You Are What You Tweet	**9 Read All About It**	**10 Assessment**
- Understand the effect of structural and grammatical devices in an article. - Evaluate the use of personal pronouns and imperatives. - Write an advice text for someone new to social networking.	- Explore how fact and opinion are combined in a review. - Identify and respond to informal and metaphorical language. - Write a review about a musical artist or their work.	- Student Book: Write a feature article about something that interests young people. - Kerboodle: Give a presentation advocating the inclusion of a particular person in a display about inspirational figures.

Preparing to teach

Refresh your knowledge

You might find it helpful to refer to the following key points when planning your teaching of this unit.

- Non-fiction can be defined as any piece of writing presented as factual (whether accurately or not). Thus, there are a multitude of non-fiction genres, such as textbooks, instruction manuals, diaries, travel writing, biographies and autobiographies, essays, journals and newspapers.

- Non-fiction writing has been in existence for many centuries, e.g. Herodotus' Histories; the Anglo-Saxon Chronicle; Doomsday Book; legal charters such as Magna Carta; political pamphlets during the Civil War; Pepys' Diaries; and church registers. The Bible is also debatably a non-fiction text. Town criers were part of the oral, pre-media, non-fiction tradition. Newspapers began in 1700, with magazines introduced later that century. Radio, TV, and the Internet made their debut in the 20th century.

- Non-fiction writing has continually evolved and expanded to encompass a wide range of forms. The Internet has greatly expanded opportunities to read and write non-fiction. Popular new online forms of non-fiction include: tweets, posts, emails, web articles, and petitions. Social networking and professional platforms have added further opportunities to 'read all about it' and publish whatever we think or feel – 24/7.

- Non-fiction is not necessarily true, accurate or factual – it is presented as true and factual. All non-fiction is produced by someone; no one can be unbiased or entirely objective, unless stating a straightforward fact, such as 'hedgehogs are prickly'.

Links and further reading

- Online newspapers, such as the following, contain much non-fiction material: www.theguardian.com, www.huffingtonpost.com, www.telegraph.co.uk, www.thetimes.co.uk.

- www.goodreads.com provides summaries of a wealth of biographies, autobiographies and other non-fiction books.

- www.amazon.co.uk can assist searches for appropriate teen non-fiction.

- www.psychologytoday.com has a wide range of articles on topical issues.

- www.bbc.co.uk/sport contains current sports news and features.

- www.bbc.co.uk/music contains current music news and features.

- Recommended non-fiction for students' independent reading: *The World According to Clarkson* by Jeremy Clarkson; *What You See is What You Get* by Alan Sugar; *The Life and Times of the Thunderbolt Kid* by Bill Bryson; *Making Happy People: The nature of happiness and its origins in childhood* by Paul Martin; *I Can't Keep My Own Secrets: Six-word Memoirs by Teens Famous and Obscure* by Larry Smith; *Steve Jobs: The Man Who Thought Different* by Karen Blumenthal; *Would You Rather?* by Chris Higgins; *Brandwashed: Tricks Companies Use to Manipulate Our Minds and Persuade Us to Buy* by Martin Lindstrom; *101 Things You Wish You'd Invented And Some You Wish No One Had* by Richard Horne and Tracey Turner; *The Vogue Factor* by Kirstie Clements; *The Kindness of Strangers: The Autobiography* by Kate Adie.

Please note that OUP is not responsible for third-party content. Although all links were correct at the time of publication, the content and location of this material may change.

Planning guidance and teaching tips

Think about how you can make the materials relevant to your students and responsive to their needs. Some suggested approaches to address key areas are provided below.

- All students are part of **the wider community** – in which they make choices and pursue non-academic interests. Consider any non-academic interests that your students might have, and how they might be starting to make responsible choices related to them.

- Remind students that they read and write non-fiction all the time – a note on the fridge, a text, a tweet, an email, an advert, or a news headline.

- Promote inclusivity by encouraging **EAL** students to use translation tools on websites – and to contribute ideas and trends from their own cultures.

- The reading age for most tabloids is nine, but higher for broadsheets. So, it might be worth **adapting some texts for less-able readers**. You can run a readability test at: http://www.online-utility.org/english/readability_test_and_improve.jsp. Remember to highlight strengths in spoken English with less-able students.

- Give students time to **read non-fiction for pleasure**, such as newspapers, autobiographies or magazines (as well as visiting different websites).

- Encourage students to **read their work aloud** and to **hear their own writing read by others**.

- Provide opportunities for students to **proofread and edit** their own writing and that of others. Set up mixed-ability editorial teams within the class.

- Aim for a wider, real-life audience by using **local and national journalism competitions** to inspire students to write their own non-fiction. Also suggest that students use their peers and school staff as an audience, e.g. through the school magazine or website.

- Open an informal dialogue with students about their work. Encourage them to counter your written comments with written comments of their own. Email them, if this facility is available in your school, and chat about their work.

- As writing within society becomes more casual, many web articles and texts now contain errors of punctuation and grammar. Encourage students to find these errors and correct them if they copy and paste web information, or download it for display.

- Refer to the **Grammar Reference Guide** on Kerboodle for definitions and exemplars of the specific grammar and punctuation terms covered in this unit, as highlighted by the Literacy Feature icon. Kerboodle also provides **SPAG interactives** to help improve the technical accuracy of students' writing and the application of grammar in context.

Lesson focus

Why are we teaching this?

The texts in this lesson are very real examples of how decisions are made about facilities for young people – and of how a lack of facilities can lead to anti-social behaviour. Many students will have strong opinions about recreational activities for young people and be able to use their own out-of-school experiences to add weight and relevance to their presentations.

What are students learning?

Students will be able to:

● discuss an issue and prepare a presentation to convey a viewpoint.

How you could teach this

A variety of activities and approaches are provided on the right for you to select from and adapt to meet the needs of your students. The Kerboodle lesson player sequence is derived from these suggestions, to act as a starting point for your lesson.

Teaching suggestions

Ignition

Ignite English interview

You might like to play Ignite Interview Film 1 to the class. In this film we are introduced to Lisa Sewards, feature writer, and her thoughts about life choices.

Resources
Kerboodle: 4 Ignite Interview Lisa Sewards Film 1

Feature

Ask students what they understand by the word 'feature'. Encourage them to think of phrases that include this word (e.g. feature film, feature artist, facial feature, geographical feature, etc.). Guide them towards the idea that a feature needs to stand out and gain attention.

Have your say

Ask students to begin by imagining that they are adults aged between 40 and 60. Ask them what facilities they think a person of that age might recommend for young people. Then ask the class how far they, answering as themselves, might agree with those ideas and why.

Exploration

Defining our terms

As an introduction to Activity 1 in the Student Book, ask students (working in pairs or small groups) to write their own definitions for the term 'anti-social behaviour'. Then compare their answers with the following: 'Anti-social behaviour is behaviour that lacks consideration for others and may cause damage to society, whether intentionally or through negligence.'

Resources
Student Book 3: Activity 1, page 84

Deduction

When students respond to Activity 2 in the Student Book, make sure that they give their reasons. To broaden out the discussion, ask them what they think the advantages are of being a teenager in the Borough of Richmond.

Resources
Student Book 3: Activity 2, page 84

Vocabulary

As a follow-up to Activity 3 in the Student Book, use the 'Varied vocabulary' worksheet on Kerboodle to encourage students to mind-map other words for: facility, good, bad, boring, interesting.

Resources
Student Book 3: Activity 3, page 84

Kerboodle: 4.1 Varied vocabulary

Answers

Answers to Student Book activities, where relevant, can be found on page 105.

and guidance

Preparing to present

As preparation for Activity 4 in the Student Book, use the 'Giving effective presentations' worksheet on Kerboodle to remind students about how to present a talk effectively, e.g. using prompt cards, making eye contact and projecting their voices.

Resources
Student Book 3: Activity 4, page 84

Kerboodle: 4.1 Giving effective presentations

Choice

The proposal in the Student Book for the new games area in Ham came out of a borough-wide consultation with young people in 2009, in which they were given a choice between the new games area or a Youth Café in the Ham Youth Centre. Out of 520 young respondents, 419 voted for the new games area. Ask students to imagine that they are one of the young people who voted for the Youth Café. Their task is to write to the council describing the kind of café they envisaged and suggesting that the council adds it to the plans for the new games area. Use the 'Youth Café proposal' worksheet on Kerboodle to structure this activity.

Resources
Kerboodle: 4.1 Youth Café proposal

The Oxygen Project

Introduce the Oxygen Project youth facility – created in Moreland, Australia – as another example of community action. Give or show students the 'What is the Oxygen Project?' worksheet on Kerboodle, which provides a transcript of Part 1 of the Project's video. Ask students to summarize what the Oxygen Committee did in the lead up to acquiring its own youth provision. Then show the video itself from the weblink below and ask students if they have any ideas for improving the facility.

Resources
Kerboodle: 4.1 What is the Oxygen Project?

Weblink: http://www.moreland. vic.gov.au/community-services/ young-people/oxygen.html

Quick fix?

Use the weblink below to show Part 2 of the Oxygen Project video (describing how the facility was built). Remind students about the saying that 'Rome wasn't built in a day' (often used by older people). Discuss the facility itself. Do students think it will work? Why/ why not? You could also ask them to write a mission statement for the centre.

Resources
Weblink: http://www.moreland. vic.gov.au/community-services/ young-people/oxygen.html

Consolidation

Presentation

In response to Activity 4 in the Student Book, students could give their presentations in small groups (with you walking around the class, listening in to the presentations and commenting on them). Alternatively, you could ask for volunteers to present their ideas formally to the class as a whole. However you arrange the presentations, encourage the audience to make notes and ask questions.

Resources
Student Book 3: Activity 4, page 84

Posts

Ask students to create posts for a social-networking site about a facility for young people that they would like to have built locally.

Lights or …

Ask students, working in pairs, to suggest three reasons why youth facilities in an area are more deserving of council funding than Christmas lights. They could then share their reasons with another pair.

Extra Time

Suggest that students prepare a digital resource to support their presentations for Activity 4.

 Weblink   Presentation   Interactive activity

Lesson focus

Why are we teaching this?

Students need to understand how different persuasive devices can be used to influence a reader and lead to changes. Online petitions are becoming an increasingly popular way of making a case. However, they need to be carefully crafted if they are to be convincing. This lesson encourages students to analyse a petition about a topic and then to use this analysis as a framework for their own online petition.

What are students learning?

Students will be able to:

- explore the use of persuasive devices in a campaign text.

How you could teach this

A variety of activities and approaches are provided on the right for you to select from and adapt to meet the needs of your students. The Kerboodle lesson player sequence is derived from these suggestions, to act as a starting point for your lesson.

Answers

Answers to Student Book activities, where relevant, can be found on page 105.

Teaching suggestions

Ignition

Lobbies

Ask students to mind-map different ways of lobbying about an issue (e.g. marches, letters, news coverage, petitions, vigils, etc.). Use the 'Forms of protest' image gallery on Kerboodle to stimulate or follow-up their responses.

Resources

Kerboodle: 4.2 Forms of protest 📷

Sign on the dotted line

As an introduction to Activity 1 in the Student Book, use the 'Petition' presentation on Kerboodle to show pupils a very basic petition. Discuss with the class why it's so important that petitions are signed – and by as many people as possible.

Resources

Student Book 3: Activity 1, page 87

Kerboodle: 4.2 Petition

Extremes of emotion

As part of their response to Activity 2 in the Student Book, show pupils three emotive words with similar meanings and ask them to rank them according to the degree of emotion they convey (e.g. painful, agonizing, excruciating).

Resources

Student Book 3: Activity 2, page 87

Exploration

Lobbying online

Follow up Activity 1 in the Student Book by using the weblink below to explore the structure and potential power of petitions in more detail.

Resources

Student Book 3: Activity 1, page 87

Weblink: http://www.gopetition. co.uk/howtowriteapetition.php 🔗

Writing a petition

Suggest that students use the model petition on page 86 of the Student Book, plus the standard petition structure outlined in Activity 1, as scaffolding for their own petitions in response to Activity 3.

Resources

Student Book 3: Activity 3, page 87

Offline effectiveness

Use the weblink below to consider whether online petitions are actually very effective – particularly with regard to the recognition of digital signatures. In the light of this information, would an old-fashioned handwritten petition be more effective in the UK?

Resources

Weblink: http://www. mediabadger.com/2012/06/ online-petitions-why-they-fail/ 🔗

and guidance

Consolidation

Commas for extra information

As a class, analyse the use of commas, on two occasions, to separate out extra information in the last long sentence of the petition on page 86 of the Student Book. Ask students to rewrite this sentence using a pair of brackets and a pair of dashes instead. Explain that there are different ways of separating extra information – and that some are more emphatic than others (e.g. brackets make a very obvious separation). You could also use the relevant part of the Grammar Reference Guide on Kerboodle to strengthen students' understanding about the use of the comma.

Resources
Kerboodle: Grammar Reference Guide (comma)

The rule of three

Ask students to investigate how and why the rule of three works. Use 'The rule of three' worksheet on Kerboodle to guide them.

Resources
Kerboodle: 4.2 The rule of three

Disused spaces

Tell students, working in pairs or small groups, to think of a disused area or facility in their neighbourhood that could be redeveloped or refurbished to provide a new facility for young people. You could then ask them to sketch a plan of it, labelled as accurately and concisely as possible, to show how they envisage it being redeveloped.

Guess it

In the context of this lesson, ask students what they think the word 'slacktivist' means. What might its opposite be?

Formal letter

As a precursor to the Extra Time activity in the Student Book, use the 'Formal letter writing' worksheet on Kerboodle to show students how to produce a formal letter. Encourage them to think carefully about what the council would say and how they would phrase it in formal Standard English.

Resources
Kerboodle: 4.2 Formal letter writing

Signing off

Ask the class to consider what the qualities of a good signature might be. Then ask students to show their current signatures to a partner and discuss what they appear to say about them. The pairs should then practise different versions of their signatures until they are happy with them.

Class vote

Ask for volunteers to read out their petitions and get the class to vote on (a) how persuasive they are, and (b) how well structured they are.

Progress Check

If you decide to use the Progress Check suggestion in the Student Book, the 'Petition Progress Check' worksheet on Kerboodle will provide a template for peer assessment. You could also ask students to include a target for future improvement.

Resources
Kerboodle: 4.2 Petition Progress Check

Extra Time

Ask students to write a formal letter from the council's Recreation Sub-Committee in response to their petition.

Lesson focus

Why are we teaching this?

Sport is a subject that underpins the daily conversations of many students, especially boys. For those students who don't engage with sport *per se*, there is nevertheless a social pressure to be physically active. This lesson encourages students to explore arguments about competition – and to grasp that argument is often made more effective through the use of counter-argument.

What are students learning?

Students will be able to:
● explore how writers present arguments and counter-arguments.

How you could teach this

A variety of activities and approaches are provided on the right for you to select from and adapt to meet the needs of your students. The Kerboodle lesson player sequence is derived from these suggestions, to act as a starting point for your lesson.

Answers

Answers to Student Book activities, where relevant, can be found on page 105.

Teaching suggestions

Ignition

Imagery

Ask students to write three similes to describe how great athletes move, e.g. 'She runs like the wind'.

Celebrity

As a follow-up to Activity 1 in the Student Book, ask students to list celebrities who have secured wealth and fame through competitive sport. Are any sports especially prominent in these lists?

Resources
Student Book 3: Activity 1, page 88

Compete

Ask students to compete to define the words 'sport' and 'competition'. Use a timer to do this.

Exploration

Reading aloud

When responding to Activities 2a and 2b in the Student Book, students might enjoy reading aloud the Jeremy Clarkson extract on page 88. Encourage them to experiment with tone and delivery, and then ask them how they think their reading aloud helps to bring out Clarkson's message about competition. The longer extract provided on Kerboodle continues the Student Book extract and could be used to help students to develop their ideas about tone and delivery.

Resources
Student Book 3: Activities 2a and 2b, page 88

Kerboodle: 4.3 Jeremy Clarkson extract continued

Manifesto

Discuss with the class the meaning of the word 'manifesto', as used in the title of the extract on page 89 of the student Book. How does it differ from 'statement' or 'outline'? Ask students to explain why Dan Travis may have chosen to use this word. Then ask which words or phrases in the extract tie in with the idea of a manifesto (guide students towards the phrases 'We should', 'Let's' and 'We need'). Finally, ask students to decide which sentence best summarises Travis' manifesto.

Resources
Student Book 3: Activity 3a, page 89

Key for Kerboodle LRA resources   Lesson Player   Image   Video    Worksheet

and guidance

Consolidation

Pros and cons

Use the 'Pros and cons' interactive activity on Kerboodle to generate student ideas and sentence starters for Activity 4 in the Student Book.

Resources

Student Book 3: Activity 4, page 89

Kerboodle: 4.3 Pros and cons

Sport in school

Set up a debate between students about whether or not the government's approach towards school sport is likely to generate future national sporting success. Use the weblinks below for background information.

Resources

Weblinks:

www.gov.uk/ (search using 'competitive sport for children')

www.independent.co.uk/ (search using 'Olympic legacy gimmick')

Keep your eye on the ball

Ask students to think of phrases that come from the world of sport. Use the 'Sports-based metaphors' worksheet on Kerboodle to focus their thinking. Ask students why these metaphors are effective.

Resources

Kerboodle: 4.3 Sports-based metaphors

Cool Britannia

Ask students to read the 'Cool Britannia' worksheet on Kerboodle, which contains a newspaper article written by Eddie Izzard in 2012 about the positive impact of the London Olympics. Then ask them to consider and respond to the questions at the end.

Resources

Kerboodle: 4.3 Cool Britannia

Expressing an opinion

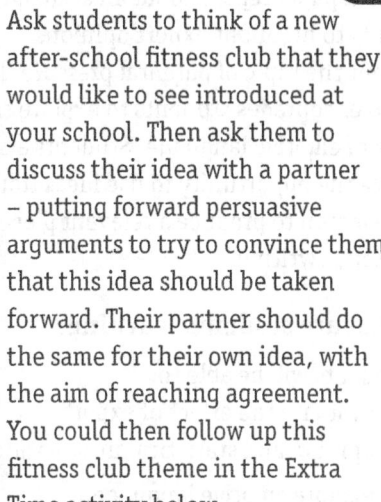

Use the 'Well-expressed arguments' worksheet on Kerboodle to help you explain to students how to argue ideas in a controlled way – avoiding words like 'love' and 'hate', and carefully using elements such as humour.

Resources

Kerboodle: 4.3 Well-expressed arguments

Join my club

Ask students to think of a new after-school fitness club that they would like to see introduced at your school. Then ask them to discuss their idea with a partner – putting forward persuasive arguments to try to convince them that this idea should be taken forward. Their partner should do the same for their own idea, with the aim of reaching agreement. You could then follow up this fitness club theme in the Extra Time activity below.

Love or hate

Ask students to express three opinions without using the phrases 'I love ...' or 'I hate ...'.

Game on?

You could ask students to discuss whether electronic gaming should be an Olympic sport (some people argue that it's no less active than shooting or archery). Ask them to make a list of reasons for and against this idea.

Extra Time

Your school has been given funds for a new after-school fitness club. Ask students to write the text for a leaflet or poster advertising this new club.

Lesson focus

Why are we teaching this?

Students need to understand how the voices and opinions of experts can be used to convince us, and how statistics can be employed to support a viewpoint or argument. This lesson uses a newspaper report about an academic study to highlight expert opinions about the topic of parental pressure. It also encourages students to explore the use of emotive language. Students also have the opportunity to use ideas from the lesson to produce a relevant piece of script writing.

What are students learning?

Students will be able to:
- evaluate the effect of expert opinion and statistical information
- explore emotive language.

How you could teach this

A variety of activities and approaches are provided on the right for you to select from and adapt to meet the needs of your students. The Kerboodle lesson player sequence is derived from these suggestions, to act as a starting point for your lesson.

Answers

Answers to Student Book activities, where relevant, can be found on page 105.

Teaching suggestions

Ignition

It's a fact

Ask each student to write down three facts about themselves and then compare them with facts written down by others in their group. Ask how we check whether something is a fact or not. Lead students towards the idea that a fact can be proved (e.g. a birth certificate can prove a person's age and date of birth, as well as their mother's maiden name and other useful details).

Loaded language

As a prelude to Activity 1b in the Student Book, ask students to write down three examples of words or phrases used by their friends, parents or teachers that tend to 'get to them'. Ask what emotion each example makes them feel (e.g. guilty, angry, sad, isolated). Explore how these words or phrases can be seen as emotive.

Resources
Student Book 3: Activity 1b, page 91

Parent power

Ask students to write down three things that their parents would probably have wanted for their future on the day they were born.

Exploration

Associations

In response to Activity 1a in the Student Book, discuss with the class what effect the quotations from the experts might have on the reader. Then ask what associations the title 'psychologist' has for students, and how the second sentence of the extract might be viewed if that word was replaced by the word 'teacher'. Then ask students to try substituting different words like 'teenager' for the word 'psychologist'. Discuss the possible effects of these changes on the reader's perceptions of and confidence in the speaker.

Resources
Student Book 3: Activity 1a, page 91

The importance of gender

Ask what further interpretations students could make from the data provided in the Student Book extract. Lead them towards the fact that most of the parents who took part in the study were mothers rather than fathers. Does this suggest that mothers are more likely to see their children as extensions of themselves?

Ignite English interview

You might like to play Ignite Interview Film 2 to the class, in which Lisa Sewards discusses writing a feature.

Resources
Kerboodle: 4 Ignite Interview Lisa Sewards Film 2

---

92 Key for Kerboodle LRA resources   Lesson Player   Image   Video  Worksheet

and guidance

Consolidation

Murray's mum

Support Activity 1c in the Student Book by showing students the newspaper article about Judy Murray on the weblink below. Discuss how far it supports the theories put forward by Professor Bushman's study. You could ask students to find evidence in the text to support Bushman's key points that parents: go to great lengths; attempt to make up for their own failed dreams; see their children as extensions of themselves; bask in the reflected glory of their children.

Resources

Student Book 3: Activity 1c, page 91

Weblink: http://www. telegraph.co.uk/sport/tennis/ andymurray/10165726/This-was-Judy-Murrays-victory-too.html

Writing headings

As a prelude to Activity 1d in the Student Book, explain that headings need to hook the reader in. Share the statistic that, on average, 8 out of 10 people will read headline copy, but only 2 out of 10 will read the rest. Then use the 'Emotive headings' presentation on Kerboodle to provide some examples of emotive headings and ask students to analyse how they hook the reader in.

Resources

Student Book 3: Activity 1d, page 91

Kerboodle: 4.4 Emotive headings

Arranged marriage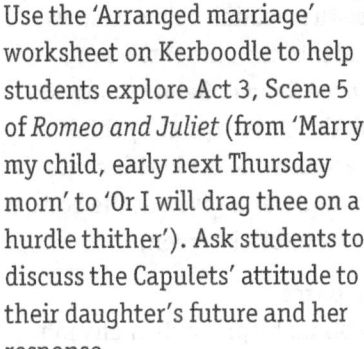

Use the 'Arranged marriage' worksheet on Kerboodle to help students explore Act 3, Scene 5 of *Romeo and Juliet* (from 'Marry my child, early next Thursday morn' to 'Or I will drag thee on a hurdle thither'). Ask students to discuss the Capulets' attitude to their daughter's future and her response.

Resources

Kerboodle: 4.4 Arranged marriage

Unhappy teenagers

Search Amazon for the description of Madeline Levine's book *The Price of Privilege*. Discuss Levine's findings with the class.

Script writing

Use the 'Good script writing' worksheet on Kerboodle to help students consider ways of making their scripts real and convincing, e.g. the use of informal language, contracted verb forms, and punctuation that suggests pauses and interruptions. Before students tackle Activity 2 in the Student Book, emphasize that they should think carefully about what the two characters would say. Suggest that they improvise the scene with a partner before they actually write their script.

Resources

Student Book 3: Activity 2, page 91

Kerboodle: 4.4 Good script writing

Opposite perspective

Ask students to imagine that they are their own parents or primary carer. Explain that their task, in role, is to write a short email to a friend about their son's/ daughter's recent achievements.

Standing up to mother

Ask student volunteers to work together in pairs to act out their scripts from Activity 4. The audience could be asked to identify all emotive language being used.

Progress Check

Distribute the 'Progress Check' worksheet on Kerboodle to help students assess their progress in understanding the features of a script.

Resources

Kerboodle: 4.4 Progress Check

Extra Time

Ask students to write a short story for the school magazine with the theme of 'Parental pressure'. They could use their scripts from Activity 4 as the basis for the story.

Lesson focus

Why are we teaching this?

This lesson uses an extract from a blog by a writer of historical fiction to enable students to explore how language can be used to engage the reader. This extract can also be used to springboard a range of reading and writing activities to explore the positives and negatives of fashion – a topic many students can readily engage with and enjoy.

What are the students learning?

Students will be able to:
- understand how writers use language to engage the reader.

How you could teach this

A variety of activities and approaches are provided on the right for you to select from and adapt to meet the needs of your students. The Kerboodle lesson player sequence is derived from these suggestions, to act as a starting point for your lesson.

Teaching suggestions

Ignition

Yankee Doodle

Use the weblink below to show students the text of the song *Yankee Doodle*. Before doing so, ask the class what they think 'macaroni' means in this context (the answer is given at the bottom of the weblink screen).

Resources
Weblink: http://kids.niehs.nih.gov/games/songs/patriotic/yankdoodmid.htm

Cartoons

Ask the class what cartoons aim to do. Then ask students, working in pairs or small groups, to create a humorous cartoon image of an extreme fashion (e.g. platform shoes), with a caption to accompany it.

Fashionable slang

List on the board five fashionable phrases currently being used by your students. Then discuss as a class how often these kinds of phrases change and how they become popular in the first place.

Exploration

Fashion language

Support Activity 1 in the Student Book by using the 'Fashion language' presentation on Kerboodle to show students a list of words/phrases that could be used to describe certain fashions. Suggest that students use these to enhance their own descriptions of fashion trends. Also explore the use of foreign words, such as 'chic', and consider why they have become popular in the fashion world. Guide students towards thinking about the international nature of fashion, and also how it can seem exotic and fashionable to use phrases from other languages.

Resources
Student Book 3: Activity 1, page 92

Kerboodle: 4.5 Fashion language

Macaroni fashion

Ask students to speculate about the origin of the word 'macaroni' in the context of the extract on page 93 of the Student Book. Discuss why those men might have been called macaronis. Then show the two different explanations in the 'Macaroni fashion' presentation on Kerboodle and ask students to decide which explanation they think provides the best fit.

Resources
Student Book 3: Activity 2a, page 93

Kerboodle: 4.5 Macaroni fashion

Answers

Answers to Student Book activities, where relevant, can be found on page 105.

and guidance

Analysing language

In response to Activity 2c in the Student Book, students could use the 'Analysing language' worksheet on Kerboodle to help them analyse the language used in the blog extract.

Resources

Student Book 3: Activity 2c, page 93

Kerboodle: 4.5 Analysing language

Is it art?

Use the weblink below to show students highlights from London Fashion Week. Ask them to debate in small groups whether these are the kinds of clothes that people could wear off the catwalk, or whether they are just 'art'? They should then decide which is the most outlandish thing they have seen and write a marketing phrase for it.

Resources

Weblink: http://www.londonfashionweek.co.uk/highlights.aspx

Zero tolerance

Ask students to read 'The Vogue Factor' worksheet on Kerboodle, which contains an extract from an article published in a newspaper Sunday supplement. Ask them to reflect on how far fashion designers and models will go in their pursuit of skeletal body sizes. Also ask them why they think so many women aspire to be so unnaturally slim.

Resources

Kerboodle: 4.5 The Vogue Factor

Facebook ready

Ask students to read and discuss the two article extracts provided as part of the 'Facebook ready' worksheet on Kerboodle, before completing the accompanying activities. What do they think the term 'Facebook ready' means?

Resources

Kerboodle: 4.5 Facebook ready

Describing a trend

To prepare for Activity 3 in the Student Book, ask students to discuss in small groups which fashion trends interest them. You could also show the 'Fashion trends' presentation on Kerboodle and students could use one of those trends as the basis for their magazine description.

Resources

Student Book 3: Activity 3, page 93

Kerboodle: 4.5 Fashion trends

Consolidation

Inventing words

If you used the first Exploration activity above, students could combine fashion words from the activity to make new words that the fashion industry might adopt.

In a nutshell

Ask students to summarize particular decades by referring to one fashion trend, e.g. 'The sixties had miniskirts'; 'The eighties had huge shoulder pads'. Encourage them to include male and multicultural fashion trends as well.

Using adjectives

Ask students to make a note of five of the adjectives used in the text and then use them to write sentences about their own wardrobes.

Extra Time

Ask students to write a school policy about the use of make-up and accessories by girls and boys. The policy needs to be realistic and not an outright ban.

 Weblink   Presentation   Interactive activity   **95**

Lesson focus

Why are we teaching this?

This lesson complements Lesson 5, because it's about how clothing is produced and the price that we're willing to pay for it – in more ways than one. Students have the opportunity to consider how writers adopt an approach or angle to a particular topic, and to develop their own ideas about how to do this.

What are students learning?

Students will be able to:
- use talk and role-play to explore complex issues.

How you could teach this

A variety of activities and approaches are provided on the right for you to select from and adapt to meet the needs of your students. The Kerboodle lesson player sequence is derived from these suggestions, to act as a starting point for your lesson.

Answers

Answers to Student Book activities, where relevant, can be found on page 105.

Teaching suggestions

Ignition

What's your angle?

Ask students if they have ever heard the phrase: 'What's your angle on this?' Then ask them to suggest some contexts where the word 'angle' might be used in this way. If they find it hard to grasp the use of this word, you could replace it with 'view' or 'take'.

Open or closed?

Ask students to write two questions that could be answered with a simple yes or no, and two questions which force the responder to say more than yes or no. This could lead to a short discussion about open and closed questions and when each is useful/not useful.

Quoting

Ask students, working in pairs, to each describe their most recent meal, and also note down one key word their partner uses. Volunteers should then feed back to the class, using a quotation gesture when repeating the exact word their partner used.

Ignite English interview

You might like to play Ignite Interview Film 2 to the class, in which Lisa Sewards discusses writing a feature.

Resources
Kerboodle: 4 Ignite Interview Lisa Sewards Film 2

Exploration

Writer's agenda

Ask students to identify any derogatory slang words and phrases, such as 'dodgy' and 'ripping-off', which have been woven into Bryony Moore's article in the Student Book. Ask them what these words and phrases tell us about Bryony's agenda. Finally, ask students to sum up in one sentence the angle the writer has taken about this subject.

Angles and viewpoints

In response to Activity 1 in the Student Book, encourage students to think about the different angles from which the news story could be approached. The writer is clearly critical of many high-street brands, but what would the brand owners want to say? How might the workers in places like Bangladesh feel about their loss of income if people in the West buy ethically produced goods instead? Ask students to identify all of the different groups and organizations mentioned in the article, before allocating a viewpoint to each one to help them prepare the interview questions. Use the 'Angles and viewpoints' worksheet on Kerboodle to help with this process.

Resources
Student Book 3: Activity 1, page 94

Kerboodle: 4.6 Angles and viewpoints

and guidance

Role-play

As preparation for their role-plays in Activity 2, remind students to:

- use open questions that will elicit more information from the interviewee
- ask about attitudes and feelings as well as events
- note down any key points the interviewee makes as a direct quotation.

Use recording devices, if available.

Resources
Student Book 3: Activity 2, page 94

Drafting

When shaping the first drafts of their articles for Activity 3, remind students that they should have:

- a clear introductory paragraph which establishes their angle
- at least two differing viewpoints, with one strong quotation from each
- a resolution of some kind, e.g. a way of improving conditions.

Resources
Student Book 3: Activity 3, page 94

Key quotations

Quotations are often used in campaigns. Ask students to choose the best quotation from their Activity 3 article to display on an ethical shopping poster.

Inside the sweatshops

Use the weblink below to show students the Channel 4 report from 27 May 2013 about Bangladeshi sweatshops. Ask them to explore the balance of the news report – how does Channel 4 ensure that different viewpoints are conveyed?

Resources
Weblink: http://www.channel4.com/news/bangladesh-inside-one-of-h-ms-biggest-clothing-factories

Oxfam fashion

Ask students to use the 'Oxfam research' worksheet on Kerboodle to help them explore the Oxfam website below, and then to review its online shopping possibilities for a fashion magazine.

Resources
Weblink: www.oxfam.org.uk

Kerboodle: 4.6 Oxfam research

Reasons to be ethical

Use the weblink below to show students the article by Jo Wood about ethical fashion. Ask them to find at least three reasons in the article to either recycle or buy ethical fashion.

Resources
Weblink: http://www.theguardian.com/lifeandstyle/2008/jul/22/jowood

Consolidation

Fashion exchange

Ask students to think about how many items of clothing they own that they don't actually wear. Explain that their task is to write an invite for a clothes exchange event to be posted on a social-networking site.

No sweat

Divide the class into pairs and ask each pair to invent a name for a new brand of ethical or up-cycled clothing. Alternatively, ask them to think of a trendy new name for a charity shop – one that would attract young people and fans of vintage clothing.

Progress Check

If you decide to use the suggestion in the Student Book, the 'Progress Check' worksheet on Kerboodle provides a template for peer assessment.

Resources
Student Book 3: page 94

Kerboodle: 4.6 Progress Check

Extra Time

Ask students to write a final draft of their article, choosing a suitable heading and including quotations to show the complexity of the issue.

Lesson focus

Why are we teaching this?

Branding is a rapidly developing and hugely powerful force in society. Students are constantly bombarded with logos, slogans and advertisements, and are very knowledgeable about brand identities. This lesson encourages them to explore attitudes to this social phenomenon and also ways of harnessing it positively.

What are students learning?

Students will be able to:
- identify how writers convey their attitude to a subject.

How you could teach this

A variety of activities and approaches are provided on the right for you to select from and adapt to meet the needs of your students. The Kerboodle lesson player sequence is derived from these suggestions, to act as a starting point for your lesson.

Teaching suggestions

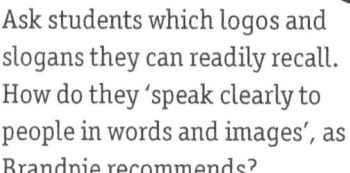

Ignition

Logo fever

Ask students which logos and slogans they can readily recall. How do they 'speak clearly to people in words and images', as Brandpie recommends?

Resources
Student Book 3: Activity 1, page 96

Human branding

Ask students to think of three different contexts for human branding. Use the 'Human branding' presentation on Kerboodle to guide them towards slavery, decoration (tattooing) and social networking.

Resources
Kerboodle: 4.7 Human branding

Choosing what to buy

Using the 'Choosing what to buy' interactive activity on Kerboodle, ask students to discuss the reasons why they choose to buy certain items of clothing and then rank them in order of importance.

Resources
Kerboodle: 4.7 Choosing what to buy

Exploration

Consumer or champion?

You could support Activity 2 in the Student Book by asking students to explore the contrast between the words 'consumer' and 'champion'. Also, look closely at how the word 'destroy' links to 'champion'. In addition, you could ask why italics are used for '*your*' and why he chooses to use the word 'relevant'.

Resources
Student Book 3: Activity 2, page 96

I.am branded

Use the weblink below to encourage students to explore Will.i.am as a brand, including his i.am camera and his partnership with companies like Coca-Cola in initiatives such as ekocycle.

Resources
Weblink:
http://will.i.am/articles/will-i-am-debuts-camera-collaboration-at-selfridges/

Brand Royal

Ask students to read and respond to the 'Brand Royal' worksheet on Kerboodle, which contains an article from the *Huffington Post* about branding lessons from the Duke and Duchess of Cambridge.

Resources
Kerboodle: 4.7 Brand Royal

Answers

Answers to Student Book activities, where relevant, can be found on page 105.

and guidance

Consolidation

The main message

Ask students to respond to Activity 3 in the Student Book by summarizing the main point of the article. Encourage them to begin by writing a topic sentence for each paragraph. Suggest that they re-read each paragraph in turn, before masking it and writing a bullet point to summarize it. When they have done this for each paragraph, get them to use their bullet points to build their short summary.

Resources
Student Book 3: Activity 3, page 97

Left to our own devices

As a class, read and discuss the poem 'The Day You Looked Me in the Eyes' by Heather Grace Stewart (provided on Kerboodle). How does this poem support Frampton's comment that brands like Apple are 'revolutionizing the way we work, play, and communicate'? Encourage students to discuss whether we are losing touch by being in touch so much.

Resources
Kerboodle: 4.7 The Day You Looked Me in the Eyes

Jesse Boot

Use the weblink below to enable students to explore the background of the philanthropist Jesse Boot (founder of Boots).

Resources
Weblink: www.spartacus. schoolnet.co.uk/BUboot.htm

Sense of identity

Give students copies of the 'Sense of identity' worksheet on Kerboodle, which includes an extract from Martin Lindstrom's book *Brand Sense* – about a boy with a bar code and the word 'GUCCI' tattooed on his neck. The brand is described in the extract as a family and a friend, but could it also be interpreted as a religion? Ask students to highlight or underline evidence in the text to support this idea.

Resources
Kerboodle: 4.7 Sense of identity

Agree or disagree?

Follow up Activity 5 in the Student Book by showing the 'Agree or disagree?' presentation on Kerboodle, which contains further opinions about brands. Again, ask students to say whether they agree or disagree with each opinion – with their reasons.

Resources
Student Book 3: Activity 5, page 97

Kerboodle: 4.7 Agree or disagree?

Plus points

Ask students to write down three positives about a brand they buy. They could present one of them as a tweet.

Slaves

Discuss the phrase 'slave to a brand'. Ask students to think of three brands they are slaves to.

Involve me

Ask students to consider and explain possible reasons why Martin Lindstrom chose to use the following quotation from Benjamin Franklin at the beginning of his book *Brand Sense*: 'Tell me and I'll forget, show me and I might remember, involve me and I'll understand.'

Extra Time

Ask students to design a questionnaire for teenagers aimed at finding out if particular brands are important to them. Emphasize that they need to think about the kinds of questions to ask, and how to contact their audience, e.g. by using SurveyMonkey.

 Weblink  Presentation   Interactive activity

Lesson focus

Why are we teaching this?

This lesson is about a preoccupation that almost every teenager shares – social networking. Although the skills focus is on structural devices within a text, this subject lends itself to the analysis of a wide range of advice and information.

What are students learning?

Students will be able to:

- understand the effect of structural and grammatical devices in an article.

How you could teach this

A variety of activities and approaches are provided on the right for you to select from and adapt to meet the needs of your students. The Kerboodle lesson player sequence is derived from these suggestions, to act as a starting point for your lesson.

Answers

Answers to Student Book activities, where relevant, can be found on page 105.

Teaching suggestions

Ignition

Follow up or introduce Activity 1 in the Student Book, by asking students to explain Facebook or Twitter to a techno-dinosaur in six bullet points or less.

Resources
Student Book 3: Activity 1, page 98

Headings

Ask students to think about (or look up, if mobiles are allowed in your classroom) the three most recent texts they sent. Their task is to give each text a heading of five words or less.

Me or you?

Ask students to write a sentence containing advice about e-safety, starting with 'You should …'. Then tell them to rewrite the sentence using 'I should …' and 'We should …'. Ask them to explain how different it feels.

Exploration

You are what you tweet

Support Activity 2 in the Student Book by asking students to explore the wordplay at work in the extract's main heading (based on 'You Are What You Eat'). Discuss other engaging headings that the author could have used for this piece. Then show the 'Engaging headings' presentation on Kerboodle and hold a class vote to select the best example.

Resources
Student Book 3: Activity 2, page 98

Kerboodle: 4.8 Engaging headings

Extra paragraphs

Ask the class how they think the Student Book extract's first paragraph hooks the reader in. Then show students the two extra sections on Kerboodle and ask them to work out where they fit best into the structure of the article. ('Don't Assume Privacy' comes before 'The Internet Is Forever', and 'Be Prepared' comes after it.) Ask students to consider how the sub-headings move the article from a sense of warning towards an optimistic resolution. Why does the author do this?

Resources
Student Book 3: Activity 2, page 98

Kerboodle: 4.8 You are what you tweet: extra sections

and guidance

Getting personal   SPAG

The author of the Student Book extract switches from 'I' to 'we' and then to 'you'. Ask students to identify where personal voice, inclusivity and direct address are used in the extract. You could ask them to find three good quotations to illustrate these devices and then to explain the effect of each one.

Resources
Student Book 3: Activity 3, page 98

Don't do that!   SPAG

Ask students to look up the meaning of the word 'imperative'. Imperatives are sometimes known as commands. Why is it sometimes imperative that we follow a command? Ask students to write a command they might use to get someone out of danger. What form of punctuation could they add to make it more urgent? You could use the Grammar Reference Guide on Kerboodle to strengthen students' understanding of the use of commands.

Resources
Student Book 3: Activity 4, page 98

Kerboodle: Grammar Reference Guide (commands)

Paris Brown

Distribute copies of the 'Paris Brown stands down' worksheet on Kerboodle. Ask students to read the newspaper article and then answer the accompanying questions about social media.

Resources
Kerboodle: 4.8 Paris Brown stands down

Writing an advice text

Before they respond to Activity 5 in the Student Book, use the 'Writing an advice text' worksheet on Kerboodle to give students some guidance. Remind them that sub-headings are useful in advice texts. Also encourage them to use imperatives of their own, and to convey solidarity through the use of collective, first-person pronouns. You could also suggest that they use a similar structure to that of the extract in the Student Book – starting with a warning and ending on a more positive note.

Resources
Student Book 3: Activity 5, page 98
Kerboodle: 4.8 Writing an advice text

Consolidation

Poetsphere

Ask students to write a post or text about a recent event they have attended. Emphasize that they should use some kind of poetic language, such as alliteration, simile or rhyme.

Defeating the object?

Show students an advert for Tweet Shirts (by searching YouTube, using the key words 'tweet shirt Xiong'). Ask them if they think this idea is likely to work. Why/ why not?

Reflecting

In the light of what they have learned this lesson, ask students to mind-map their priorities for personal branding and social-networking behaviour with a partner.

Extra Time

Ask students to write a short story or poem using one of the following sayings as its title:

- Skeletons in the cupboard.
- It came back to haunt me.
- The past caught up with me.

They could use the story of Paris Brown as the basis for their ideas.

Lesson focus

Why are we teaching this?

Students are bound to have strong connections with music and this lesson focuses on the use of facts and opinions in music reviews. It also primes students for writing a feature article, thus preparing them for the end-of-unit assessment.

What are students learning?

Students will be able to:

- explore how fact and opinion are combined in a review.

How you could teach this

A variety of activities and approaches are provided on the right for you to select from and adapt to meet the needs of your students. The Kerboodle lesson player sequence is derived from these suggestions, to act as a starting point for your lesson.

> **Answers**
>
> Answers to Student Book activities, where relevant, can be found on page 105.

Teaching suggestions

Ignition

Fact

As an introduction to Activity 2a in the Student Book, ask students to list three facts about their favourite musicians. They then have to take each fact in turn and explain exactly how it could be proved (e.g. using a birth certificate to prove a person's birthday and age).

Resources
Student Book 3: Activity 2a, page 100

Jamming

Play a video of Bob Marley's *Jamming* from YouTube. Ask students what adjectives they would use to describe it.

Identifying opinions

Using the 'Identifying opinions' interactive activity on Kerboodle, discuss each statement to ensure that students understand the difference between opinion and fact.

Resources
Kerboodle: 4.9 Identifying opinions

Ignite English interview

You might like to play Ignite Interview Film 1 to the class. In this film we are introduced to Lisa Sewards and her thoughts about life choices.

Resources
Kerboodle: 4 Ignite Interview Lisa Sewards Film 1

Exploration

Connotations

When exploring the adjectives used in the Bob Marley review, lead students towards identifying the words *inventive*, *honeyed* and *powerful*. Use the 'Connotations' presentation on Kerboodle to explain that connotations are simply the associations we have with words. Note that the reviewer uses two very overused adjectives – lovely and great. Ask students to replace these with more precise and exciting adjectives.

Resources
Student Book 3: Activity 2b, page 100

Kerboodle: 4.9 Connotations

Summarize

Ask students to summarize their own favourite musician and their music in a single powerful sentence – that includes some well-considered adjectives.

Resources
Student Book 3: Activity 2c, page 100

Nice work

Explore with the class the writer's use of the words 'nice' and 'nicely' in the Emeli Sandé review. Do students think that these words have been used for want of better vocabulary, or are they part of a very deliberate craft? What might the writer intend by using them?

and guidance

Fact and opinion

When exploring the use of fact and opinion in the Emeli Sandé review, ask students to note the use of the facts – the number of nights and the venue capacity – and how they suggest Sandé's popularity. Pick out the phrases 'Of course' and 'I wanted to reply', both of which convey the writer's opinion.

Resources
Student Book 3: Activity 3a, page 102

Slang

Ask students to list acceptable slang words associated with music and the music industry.

Informal or slang?

Before asking students to tackle Activity 3b, you may need to explain the difference between formal and informal language. Ask them to consider if any of the informal words are slang. Using these examples, can students explain the difference between informal language and slang? You could use the 'Informal language or slang' worksheet on Kerboodle to help.

Resources
Student Book 3: Activity 3b, page 102

Kerboodle: 4.9 Informal language or slang

Metaphors

As part of their response to Activity 3c in the Student Book, explore with students the extended 'bread and jam' metaphor in the Emeli Sandé review. The 'Metaphors' worksheet on Kerboodle contains specific questions about the use of metaphors in this review.

Resources
Student Book 3: Activity 3c, page 102

Kerboodle: 4.9 Metaphors

More on Emeli Sandé

Ask students to read the additional article about Emeli Sandé provided on Kerboodle and answer the accompanying questions.

Resources
Kerboodle: 4.9 Emeli Sandé article

Writing your review

Before they tackle Activity 4 in the Student Book, suggest that students mind-map their review in four boxes or circles. Ask them to include: relevant facts; key adjectives that describe this musician or type of music; informal phrases associated with this musician or music; words which convey their own opinion.

Resources
Student Book 3: Activity 4, page 102

Consolidation

Review of reviews

Ask volunteers to read out their reviews from Activity 4. Ask the audience to identify one thing they like about the review's use of language and one thing that could be improved.

Talent shows

Discuss programmes like *The Voice* and *X-Factor* with the class. Do they ever produce artists like Emeli Sandé and Bob Marley? Ask each student to give a one-sentence answer. Also say that, before the next speaker continues the discussion, they have to identify whether the previous speaker used a fact or an opinion.

Too old?

Ask students how they feel about older people attending gigs. Ask them to write down three reasons why someone over 50 should see their favourite artist or band. Award extra marks to anyone who can use an extended metaphor.

Extra Time

Ask students to plan the vocabulary for a tag cloud (word cloud) to appear on the website of a musician of their choice.

Assessment focus

Why are we assessing this?

Students have completed a unit on non-fiction and explored a wide range of forms and topics. By analysing a variety of texts and undertaking written tasks, students should have developed their skills as authors and practised using the elements of good writing. They will have noticed what engages a reader and how styles of writing convey different angles and attitudes. Discussion, reading and writing should have helped them to develop a strong sense of audience and purpose.

What are students demonstrating?

Students will be able to:

- write a feature article for a new website on a subject of their choice that would be interesting to young people.

How to deliver the assessment

Suggestions and guidance on how to set up and prepare your students for the assessment are provided as well as possible approaches to marking the assessment.

Alternative/additional assessment

There is an alternative end-of-unit assessment available on Kerboodle. This assessment leads to a spoken English outcome and can be used either in addition to or instead of the Student Book end-of-unit assessment.

Resources
Kerboodle: 4.10 Alternative end-of-unit assessment

Assessment suggestions and guidance

Understanding the assessment

Check that students understand the assessment task set. Emphasize that they are being tested on their *writing* skills.

Resources
Student Book 3: pages 104–105

Reading and planning

Remind students that they first need to plan their articles carefully. Emphasize that they should take care to select subject matter that will enable them to produce a sustained response. Encourage them to include elements typical in a feature article, such as quotations, acceptable informal language or expert opinion. Inform students that these can be invented. Also emphasize the importance of careful structure, grammar and punctuation.

Completing the assessment

Remind students of the form that their assessment should take, i.e. writing a feature article. Emphasize that students must complete the assessment individually, so that an accurate mark or level can be given.

Timing and writing expectation

Give students one hour (ideally one lesson) and expect between one and two A4 pages.

Marking

You will want to mark this in line with departmental and school marking guidelines. If you wish, you could use the Ignite English marking scales provided on Kerboodle. Using the Ignite English marking scales will help you to identify specific strengths and areas for improvement in an individual student's writing. This may help you to set development targets as well as build a profile of your class as writers.

Refer to the KS3 National Curriculum and Ignite English mapping grids on pages 154–156 of this Teacher Companion to identify other Ignite English units where these writing skills are covered, or ask students to use the SPAG interactives on Kerboodle to address any areas identified for improvement. The Grammar Reference Guide on Kerboodle contains definitions and additional examples of each of the spelling, punctuation and grammar points covered in the interactives, for your reference.

Resources
Kerboodle: 4 Ignite English marking scales

Kerboodle: SPAG interactives

Kerboodle: Grammar Reference Guide

Key for Kerboodle LRA resources   Worksheet   Interactive activity

Student Book answers

Below are the answers to any largely non-subjective Student Book activities contained within this unit.

Lesson 3

3a Arguments for competitive sport:

- It is more meaningful.
- It rewards children.
- It generates a sense of pride and it teaches them to deal equally with success and failure.

3b He counters the argument by saying 'a temporary loss of self-esteem will not cause permanent damage to children'.

Lesson 4

1b Emotive words or phrases: 'pushy'; 'forced to endure'; 'failed dreams'; 'egging ... on'; 'lost dreams'; 'reflected glory'; 'regret'; 'disappointment'.

1c The anecdote helps to illustrate the point because it's about a famous example of parental pressure. The anecdote mirrors what the study has revealed.

Lesson 5

2b 'absurd', 'shock', 'copious', 'outrageous', 'gaudy', 'showy', 'elaborate'

Lesson 8

1 'Tweet' originally meant the chirp of a young bird and 'twitter' meant a series of short birdcalls.

3 'I', 'we' and 'you'

4 'take advantage of' and 'don't put'

Lesson 9

2a Facts:

- Marley recorded some of his music in London.
- He was the victim of a murder attempt.
- Three of the tracks became international hits.

2b 'powerful', 'inspired', 'irresistible'

3b Informal language: 'gigs', 'bagged', 'a bit on', 'jamminess', 'spouting', 'thwackier', 'disser'

3d The prefix 'dis' acts as a negative or reversing force on words, e.g. like/dislike.

Unit 5: Young Entrepreneurs

Unit overview

Why are we teaching this?

The arrival on screen of entrepreneurial TV shows, such as *Dragons' Den* and *The Apprentice*, has provided teachers with an alternative and effective way of combining **spoken, written and group-work skills** with **motivating activities**. The activities in this unit, drawn from real-life situations, are engaging and appealing. Many students will go on to **start a business**, whilst others will become essential **employees** in new businesses. The English skills in this unit will support those ambitions and **improve employability**. Sound **literacy skills** are essential for creating a successful business.

What are the learning aims?

By the end of the unit, students will be able to:

- select relevant information, using inference, from a variety of non-fiction texts
- understand and use specialist vocabulary confidently in order to plan and discuss business concepts
- identify and use appropriate levels of formality in writing, depending on the audience and context
- understand how to select vocabulary and craft phrases in order to create a specific reaction in the target audience
- employ techniques for effective listening, questioning and responding to others during role-play
- use verbal and non-verbal techniques in spoken presentations.

How will this be assessed?

Key assessment task	Focus for assessment
Student Book: Using spoken English skills, and knowledge gained about business, to pitch an idea for a new business to two potential investors.	- Demonstrating good spoken English skills.
Kerboodle: Writing a pitch to persuade investors to invest in a particular business idea.	- Writing a polished pitch, creating an appropriately formal tone and drawing on rhetorical devices for persuasive effect. - Structuring the pitch effectively. - Using a range of vocabulary, sentence structures and punctuation precisely.

The end-of-unit assessment on Kerboodle can be used either instead of or in addition to the Student Book end-of-unit assessment.

Note that short Progress Checks also feature in this unit, providing formative assessment opportunities to support students' learning.

Lesson sequence

This is a suggested lesson sequence, but you might choose to alter or add to it to suit your particular teaching needs.

Introducing the unit

1 Gap in the Market

- Explore the qualities and skills needed to be a successful businessperson.
- Respond to the Ignite interview, featuring Renée Watson.
- Select relevant information, using inference, from a variety of non-fiction texts.

2 Choosing the Big Idea	3 Planning your New Business	4 Levels of formality
• Make a sustained contribution to group discussion, listening carefully, asking relevant questions, exploring and developing their own ideas and those of other people. • Engage in sustained group work to develop possible business ideas for a pitch. • Respond to peer assessment of speaking and listening skills.	• Understand and use specialist vocabulary confidently in order to plan and discuss business concepts. • Learn key business terms and concepts from Kanya King's interview. • Use cross-curricular skills to develop financial and marketing ideas for the pitch.	• Identify and use appropriate levels of formality in writing, depending on audience and context. • Explore levels of formality through analysing a letter by Richard Branson. • Write a formal letter to a potential investor.
5 Names and Associations	6 Premises and Finance	7 Personality Sells
• Understand how to select vocabulary and craft phrases in order to create a specific reaction. • Use the example of James Caan's company to consider the connotations of business names. • Create an appropriate name for a company's target audience.	• Explore techniques to summarize and present information clearly and concisely. • Write a clear and concise 'wanted' advert. • Develop a financial plan and summarize it clearly and concisely for potential investors.	• Explore the use of verbal and non-verbal techniques to promote and sell a product. • Analyse the use of verbal and non-verbal techniques in Levi Roots' pitch for *Dragons' Den*. • Create a mini pitch for a marketplace using verbal and non-verbal techniques.
8 Responding to Questions	9 Preparing the pitch	10 Assessment
• Develop techniques for effective listening, questioning and responding to others during role-play. • Role-play an interview with another student. • Learn from peer assessment of the interview.	• Analyse a successful pitch, noting techniques that are effective and can be used for other pitches. • Prepare a pitch using effective planning, drafting and rehearsing techniques.	• Student Book: As a group, divided up into different roles, present a formal business pitch with confidence and enthusiasm. • Kerboodle: Writing a pitch to persuade investors to invest in a particular business idea.

Preparing to teach

Refresh your knowledge

You might find it helpful to refer to the following key points when planning your teaching of this unit.

- The term 'entrepreneur' was first used by the economist Richard Cantillon in 1734 (in brief, meaning somebody who does not earn a fixed income). Literally, it means 'undertaker'. However, the definition of entrepreneur has developed and changed as theorists and educational institutions have analysed the development of business. The current Oxford Dictionary definition is: 'a person who sets up a business or businesses, taking on financial risks in the hope of profit'.

- The study of entrepreneurs and their businesses has become popular, as new entrepreneurs attempt to emulate others' successes. A successful entrepreneur is often seen as an innovator who takes informed risks to start, lead and maintain a successful business. Entrepreneurs are said to grasp opportunities and be prepared to accept failure. Many autobiographies and websites, such as those listed below, will reinforce your background knowledge for this unit.

- It is well worth watching TV shows, such as *The Apprentice* and *Dragons' Den,* to glean information about what makes a good investment and what entrepreneurs are looking for in a new business opportunity.

- The terms 'unique selling point', 'financial viability' and 'target market' may be very familiar to you. However, if not, check through the glossaries in the Student Book to refresh your memory.

- There are many startup websites with example pitches. Also, YouTube provides many TV show examples and other pitches.

Links and further reading

- James Caan: http://www.james-caan.com/
- Young Apprentice: http://www.bbc.co.uk/programmes/b016kgww
- Levi Roots: http://www.leviroots.com/
- Mobo awards: http://www.mobo.com/
- Information on Kanya King: http://www.womenspeakers.co.uk/speakerprofile/69/Kanya%20King
- Business Startup website http://www.startups.co.uk/

- Recommended works for students' independent reading: *Common Sense Rules* by Deborah Meaden; *Bold As Brass* by Hilary Devey; *Losing My Virginity The Autobiography* by Richard Branson; *Start your Business in 7 Days* by James Caan; *You Can Get It If You Really Want* by Levi Roots; *What You See is What You Get, My Autobiography* by Alan Sugar.

Please note that OUP is not responsible for third-party content. Although all links were correct at the time of publication, the content and location of this material may change.

Planning guidance and teaching tips

Think about how you can make the materials relevant to your students and responsive to their needs. Some suggested approaches to address key areas are provided below.

- As the end-of-unit assessment is a spoken pitch, take every opportunity to develop students' **confidence to speak** – particularly those students who do not usually volunteer to speak in class, because they will need to speak in front of others in the final pitch. Use paired work before encouraging students to feed back to the whole class. Also, use the random name generator to encourage all students to speak (http://www.superteachertools.com/instantclassroom/random-name-generator.php). Alternatively, ask students to write their names on cards, which you can then shuffle to select students at random.

- You need to decide early on whether students will present their final pitch entirely **on their own** in Lesson 10, or **as part of a group**. This will depend on your class. If students are working in a group, emphasize that every student should present part of the final pitch. In the following activities, it has been assumed that a group pitch will be adopted for the final assessment, with a large enough role taken by each student to allow their spoken English skills to be assessed.

- Spoken English skills can be assessed continually throughout this unit. However, the end-of-unit assessment evaluates students' ability to **speak formally** in a more-challenging situation (a business pitch in front of potential investors).

- **Autobiographies** of business entrepreneurs, such as those listed opposite, are a great way to get many students reading. Challenge them to read about someone they are interested in. Ask the librarian to display relevant autobiographies and business texts during the unit.

- **EAL students** benefit greatly from the use of spoken language and group work in class. If they are only just beginning to speak English, ask other students to include them by getting them to demonstrate props or read out key information from cards during mini-presentations and pitches. This unit includes the use of pictures. Refer to the key words that go with these pictures and write them on the board. Use the kinaesthetic activities, so that they can see and copy what other students do.

- Model speech and activities at the front of the class for **lower-attaining students**. You could model activities yourself, or ask other students to model tasks. You could give some students the homework of preparing to demonstrate something in the following lesson. Give able and confident students the chance to lead and encourage others to follow suit.

- Refer to the **Grammar Reference Guide** on Kerboodle for definitions and exemplars of the specific grammar and punctuation terms covered in this unit, as highlighted by the Literacy Feature icon. Kerboodle also provides **SPAG interactives** to help improve the technical accuracy of students' writing and the application of grammar in context.

- You could use the Ignite Interview with Renée Watson in the Student Book, or play the Ignite Interview films on Kerboodle to introduce the topic.

Lesson focus

Why are we teaching this?

In this lesson, students learn about the skills and qualities needed to be a successful businessperson – at the same time as developing their own inference skills. The skills and qualities inferred from the extracts in this lesson will support students' preparation for a successful pitch in the end-of-unit assessment. Additionally, students are learning qualities from role models who reflect positive attitudes, such as teamwork and determination – essential skills for both successful learners and business people.

What are students learning?

Students will be able to:
- use inference to select information from non-fiction texts.

How you could teach this

A variety of activities and approaches are provided on the right for you to select from and adapt to meet the needs of your students. The Kerboodle lesson player sequence is derived from these suggestions, to act as a starting point for your lesson.

Answers

Answers to Student Book activities, where relevant, can be found on page 129.

Teaching suggestions

Ignition

Ignite English interview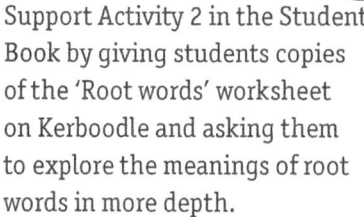

You might like to play Ignite Interview Film 1 to the class. In this film we are introduced to Renée Watson, business founder and owner, and her thoughts about creating a business.

Resources

Kerboodle: 5 Ignite Interview Renée Watson Film 1

Prior knowledge

Ask students to use their existing knowledge to list the key qualities and skills of a successful businessperson of their choice. This task could be completed after a famous entrepreneur's skills and qualities have been discussed as an example. You could also ask students to work in pairs before feeding back to the rest of the class.

Resources

Student Book 3: Activity 1, page 107

Ranking skills and qualities

Ask students to use the 'Ranking skills and qualities' worksheet on Kerboodle to rank, in order of importance, the skills and qualities they identified in the 'Prior knowledge' activity. (There are no correct answers, but students should be asked to justify their decisions.)

Resources

Kerboodle: 5.1 Ranking skills and qualities

Exploration

A local gap in the market

Ask students to picture a local high street or shopping centre that they know personally. If they were going to rent a business premises in that location, what service or business would be successful there, in their view? Ask for volunteers to feed back their ideas and explain their reasoning.

Root words

Support Activity 2 in the Student Book by giving students copies of the 'Root words' worksheet on Kerboodle and asking them to explore the meanings of root words in more depth.

Resources

Student Book 3: Activity 2, page 108

Kerboodle: 5.1 Root words

Reading and inference

Encourage students to respond to Activity 3 in the Student Book by using inference to work out the skills and qualities displayed by the entrepreneurs in the two extracts. You could start them off by discussing the following example from the Richard Branson extract: 'I thought about the high cost of records …', which shows that he was aware of financial implications and the target market.

Resources

Student Book 3: Activity 3, page 108

and guidance

Consolidation

Paired reading

Divide the class into pairs and ask them to make inferences from each sentence in the two extracts. For example, one student could read out the first sentence of the Kanya King extract ('Today she [Kanya King] has plenty to smile about'), while the other student infers from it that King is happy and successful. Tell them to swap roles for the Branson extract.

Resources
Student Book 3: Activity 3, page 108

Gaps in the market

You could support students by rephrasing Activity 4 in the Student Book in a simpler form. For example, 'What business opportunities did the two entrepreneurs see?' or 'What did Branson and King want to give people that no other company had?'

Resources
Student Book 3: Activity 4, page 108

Deadly duo

Tell students to imagine that Richard Branson and Kanya King have decided to work together on a business venture. Using inference and the two Student Book extracts, ask them to decide what business idea the two entrepreneurs should pursue – based on their skills, experience and knowledge. Also ask students to describe, with reasons, the roles that each entrepreneur should take in the business.

Extra Time

Ask students to do some research about another successful entrepreneur and find out what gap in the market they decided to fill. You could give some support by asking them to use relevant autobiographies from the library, or to look up information on the Internet. Give examples of people they may wish to research, such as: James Caan, Kanya King, Karen Brady, Deborah Meaden, Lord Sugar, Simon Cowell, Hilary Devey, Steve Jobs, etc.

Inferring evidence

Ask students to write down two things that were obvious about Branson and King from the Student Book extracts, before adding two things that had to be worked out by inference from the text.

Kinaesthetic

Divide the class into pairs and ask students to take it in turns to show each other the entrepreneurial skills and qualities that they inferred from the two Student Book extracts – using only actions (no speaking). Explain that they have to try to guess which skill or quality their partner is illustrating. Ask two students to take part in a demonstration at the front of the class before beginning the activity.

Using inference

Put the following quotation in the centre of a spider diagram and ask students to prove to you that they can use inference by noting as many things as they can about Kanya King only using the quotation. 'She had been knocking on many doors.' Suggested inferences: determination, finds contacts, communication with others, self-belief, confidence.

Lesson focus

Why are we teaching this?

In this lesson students will develop their group-work and listening skills in preparation for the end-of-unit assessment. It is also an opportunity for them to explore creativity through speaking, listening and business skills, as they share and begin to develop their business ideas for the big pitch at the end of the unit.

What are students learning?

Students will be able to:

- make a sustained contribution to group discussion, listening carefully, asking relevant questions, exploring and developing their own ideas and those of other people.

How you could teach this

A variety of activities and approaches are provided on the right for you to select from and adapt to meet the needs of your students. The Kerboodle lesson player sequence is derived from these suggestions, to act as a starting point for your lesson.

> **Answers**
>
> Answers to Student Book activities, where relevant, can be found on page 129.

Teaching suggestions

Ignition

Brainstorming

Ask students to list all of the businesses they can think of. Then ask them to choose three businesses from their lists that they would like to have created.

Who is the ...?

Divide the class into small groups and ask them to discuss and decide who they think the most successful businessperson in the UK is. Once they have decided, ask them to assess who spoke the most during the group discussion and who might be called the group leader. Could anyone have spoken more?

Exploration

Business area

Timings in this lesson could be difficult to judge, depending on how quickly students focus their ideas. Give time limits and keep reassessing how much time is needed. Once they have decided on their preferred business area in Activity 1, students should form suitable groups to take it forward during the rest of the unit. Instead of students choosing their groups, you could ask each one to write their name and preferred business area on a card, so that you can group and shuffle the cards to distribute the students randomly, or as you decide. Group them by business area, because they will be working on this particular area for their end-of-unit pitch.

Resources
Student Book 3: Activity 1, page 110

Ideas for your business

In order to help generate suitable ideas for a business venture, display the 'Prompt questions' presentation on Kerboodle, or print it out and give it to those groups who need more support.

Resources
Student Book 3: Activity 2, page 111

Kerboodle: 5.2 Prompt questions

and guidance

Note taking

Explain that students need to make notes on all of their business ideas to refer back to later. Encourage them to use their preferred method of note taking: mind-map, diagram, table, list, etc.

Resources
Student Book 3: Activity 3, page 111

Narrowing down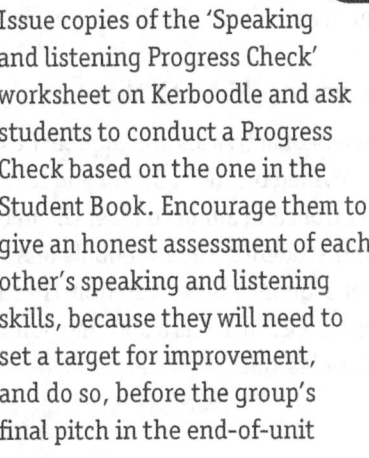

Ask each group to reduce their business ideas down to three, by considering the three bullet points in Activity 4. Before they do this, you might want to draw their attention to the key terms 'target market' and 'USP' (unique selling point). Write them on the board and check students' understanding. Each group should then complete Activity 5 by voting on the best business idea to take forward. Emphasize that this idea will then be their group's focus for the rest of the unit, so it's an important group decision.

Resources
Student Book 3: Activities 4–5, page 111

Strengths and weaknesses

Ask students to write down all of the strengths and weaknesses of their chosen business idea up to this point. They should then talk them through, listening carefully to each other, so that they can try to find a solution to any weaknesses.

An example clip

You could show a clip from 'The Young Apprentice', where contestants are planning for a task. Tell students to assess one of the contestants on the same speaking and listening criteria as those in the Student Book Progress Check.

Ignite English interview

You might like to play Ignite Interview Film 1 to the class. In this film we are introduced to Renée Watson and her thoughts about creating a business.

Resources
Kerboodle. 5 Ignite Interview Renée Watson Film 1

Extra Time

Ask students to complete a SWOT analysis for their group's business idea. What are the strengths, weaknesses, opportunities and threats for their proposed business? (Opportunities = What will be gained by the customer and the staff? Threats = What could go wrong?)

Consolidation

Retell

Ask students to explain their group's business idea to somebody in a different group, before listening to that group's idea. They should then ask each other two questions about their proposed businesses, so that they can develop their ideas further when they return to their own group.

Progress Check

Issue copies of the 'Speaking and listening Progress Check' worksheet on Kerboodle and ask students to conduct a Progress Check based on the one in the Student Book. Encourage them to give an honest assessment of each other's speaking and listening skills, because they will need to set a target for improvement, and do so, before the group's final pitch in the end-of-unit assessment.

Resources
Student Book 3: Progress Check, page 111

Kerboodle: 5.2 Speaking and listening Progress Check

Lesson focus

Why are we teaching this?

Students will often need to learn a new set of words, or jargon, for each new situation, school subject or job they encounter. This lesson teaches them the key words for this topic, as well as the ability to understand key words from reading and how to use those words in discussion. The lesson also fosters the ability to incorporate skills from different areas of the curriculum (Maths, Business and English). This use of connections and links is important, not only in English but in the skills of learning.

What are students learning?

Students will be able to:

- understand and use specialist vocabulary confidently in order to plan and discuss business concepts.

How you could teach this

A variety of activities and approaches are provided on the right for you to select from and adapt to meet the needs of your students. The Kerboodle lesson player sequence is derived from these suggestions, to act as a starting point for your lesson.

Answers

Answers to Student Book activities, where relevant, can be found on page 129.

Teaching suggestions

Ignition

Race to list key words

Ask students to write down as many business-related key words or phrases as they can in three minutes. Ask the student with the longest list to share their key words with the rest of the class and use it to check understanding.

Explain the diagram

Show the 'Diagram of business' presentation on Kerboodle and ask students to both explain it and identify which specialist terms are being used.

Resources
Kerboodle: 5.3 Diagram of business

Odd one out

Ask students to decide on the odd one out from the following list of words: remortgage, debit, credit, loan. They may identify credit as the odd one out, because it's the only one that does not involve borrowing money. However, accept any answer that is supported with a good reason.

Exploration

Key terms and definitions

Encourage students to use the context to work out the meanings of the underlined words/phrases in the Kanya King interview. If required, direct students to a suitable dictionary.

Resources
Student Book 3: Activity 1 page 112

The importance of jargon

Hand out copies of the 'Jargon' worksheet on Kerboodle and ask students to work through it to help them understand the concept of jargon and why it's important to understand specialist terms.

Resources
Kerboodle: 5.3 Jargon

Comprehension of business terms

Answering Activities 2a and 2b in the Student Book, about raising finance and the promotion of Kanya King's business idea, requires close reading of the extract. This will help students to understand the key terms in context. If appropriate, also encourage them to tackle the stretch task.

Resources
Student Book 3: Activities 2a and 2b, page 113

and guidance

Consolidation

Mini-feedback presentation planning

The activities and tips on pages 114–115 of the Student Book will help students to frame and develop their ideas about finance and marketing. They will also provide an opportunity for students to practise their speaking and listening skills before the final end-of-unit pitch. You could hold the two mini-presentations at the beginning of the next lesson, giving students in each sub-group more time to plan.

Resources
Student Book 3: Activities 3–4, page 114

Accounting role-play

Tell students that they have to get together with their accountant for a brief meeting. Divide each group into pairs and explain that their task is to role-play this meeting – with one student in each pair playing the accountant and the other the businessperson. Ask them to cover the following three questions:

- What will you spend your money on?
- How much money do you think you will get back?
- How will you advertise your business?

This task will develop their use of the key terms.

Cloze exercise

Ask students to complete the 'Key words' worksheet on Kerboodle, which is a cloze exercise about the key words used in this lesson.

Resources
Kerboodle: 5.3 Key words

Wordplay

Challenge students to race in pairs to use six key words from this lesson or the unit so far (in the context of starting a theme park, a restaurant, or a band). Ask them to underline the key terms, so you can check their understanding easily.

Ignite English interview

You might like to play Ignite Interview Film 1 to the class. In this film we are introduced to Renée Watson and her thoughts about creating a business.

Resources
Kerboodle: 5 Ignite Interview Renée Watson Film 1

Extra Time

As an example of their advertising, you could ask students to design a persuasive leaflet to give out during their final end-of-unit pitch. Emphasize that they should include persuasive devices and also make sure that it's aimed properly at their target market.

Just a minute

Ask a student volunteer to come to the front of the class and model talking about one of the lesson's key words for a minute – but without hesitating or repeating themselves. If they succeed, they win a point. Students can then compete in pairs once they are clear about the rules.

Explain the diagram revisited

If you used the 'Explain the diagram' Ignition activity, display the diagram again and ask students to talk about it in the light of their work this lesson. Check to see whether they now use more specialist terms than at the beginning of the lesson.

Resources
Kerboodle: 5.3 Diagram of business

Check the finances

Ask students to list different ways of raising money for a business. This will check their understanding of many of the key words used in this lesson.

Lesson focus

Why are we teaching this?

Students need to be able to read and write texts of increasing complexity – and with different levels of formality – within the contexts of school, work and life in general. This lesson reminds them of the need to use different levels of formality with different people. It will also make them more aware of the level of formality they need to use in the final end-of-unit pitch.

What are students learning?

Students will be able to:

- identify and use appropriate levels of formality in writing, depending on audience and context.

How you could teach this

A variety of activities and approaches are provided on the right for you to select from and adapt to meet the needs of your students. The Kerboodle lesson player sequence is derived from these suggestions, to act as a starting point for your lesson.

Teaching suggestions

Ignition

Communication

Ask students, working in pairs, to use their existing knowledge to list the different ways in which people communicate in business. Once they have compiled their list, they should rearrange the different ways from the least to the most formal.

Informal to formal

Ask students to rewrite several informal sentences into formal ones. For example: 'Alright, mate. I really wants to be the next big thing. Got any cash you can lend?'

Exploration

Spot the informal words

After reading the Branson extract on page 116 of the Student Book, ask students to respond to Activity 1 by finding evidence of informality in the letter. Give an example or two if necessary.

Resources
Student Book 3: Activity 1, page 117

Potential investor

Support Activity 2 in the Student Book by encouraging students to discuss in pairs how the language and layout used by a businessperson in a letter to a potential investor would be different to those used in a letter to a family member or friend (such as Richard Branson's father). You could use the 'A formal letter' worksheet on Kerboodle during student feedback.

Resources
Student Book 3: Activity 2, page 117

Kerboodle: 5.4 A formal letter

What's needed?

Ask students to draw a diagram, using boxes, to show what is needed in a formal letter.

Answers

Answers to Student Book activities, where relevant, can be found on page 129.

Key for Kerboodle LRA resources Lesson Player Image Video  Worksheet

and guidance

Consolidation

Planning the letter

Ensure that students plan their formal letter to a potential investor in response to Activity 3 in the Student Book. Use the worksheet on Kerboodle to remind them about the language and layout/presentation required.

Resources

Student Book 3: Activity 3, page 117

Kerboodle: 5.4 A formal letter

Example letter

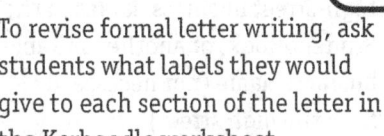

To revise formal letter writing, ask students what labels they would give to each section of the letter in the Kerboodle worksheet.

Resources

Kerboodle: 5.4 A formal letter

Label a letter

Ask students to pair up and complete the Progress Check in the Student Book by labelling each other's letters to check that their partner has used everything required in a formal letter (as outlined in the bullet points in the Progress Check panel).

Resources

Student Book 3: Progress Check, page 117

Progress Check

Use the Student Book and/or 'Formal letter assessment' worksheet on Kerboodle to make sure that all students peer assess each other's work and also set targets to improve their own formal letter-writing skills.

Resources

Student Book 3: Progress Check page 117

Kerboodle: 5.4 Formal letter assessment

Degrees of formality

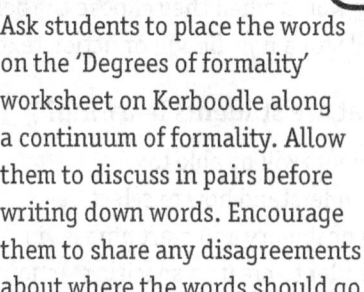

Ask students to place the words on the 'Degrees of formality' worksheet on Kerboodle along a continuum of formality. Allow them to discuss in pairs before writing down words. Encourage them to share any disagreements about where the words should go and their final decisions.

Resources

Kerboodle: 5.4 Degrees of formality

Mini-lesson

Recap the learning in the lesson by dividing the class into pairs and asking one student in each pair to spend 3 minutes teaching their partner about the presentation of formal letters. Then the two students should swap roles and the second student should spend 3 minutes teaching their partner about formal words that could be used in a business context.

Top three tips

Ask students, working in pairs, to take turns explaining their top three tips for writing in formal language. Choose several pairs to feed back their ideas to the class.

Extra Time

Richard Branson's early business idea was unsuccessful, because he had too many budgerigars and not enough customers. Ask students to find another example of a successful businessperson who had an earlier business failure. For support, you could suggest that students type 'famous successful business failure' into a search engine.

🔗 Weblink   🖥 Presentation   🔲 Interactive activity

Lesson focus

Why are we teaching this?

Creativity is valuable in both Business and English lessons. Students need to be able to choose new and relevant company names for their target audience in the same creative way as they would when they choose the best words for a non-fiction or fiction text.

What are students learning?

Students will be able to:

- understand how to select vocabulary and craft phrases in order to create a specific reaction in the target reader.

How you could teach this

A variety of activities and approaches are provided on the right for you to select from and adapt to meet the needs of your students. The Kerboodle lesson player sequence is derived from these suggestions, to act as a starting point for your lesson.

> **Answers**
>
> Answers to Student Book activities, where relevant, can be found on page 129.

Teaching suggestions

Ignition

Comfort or Strength

Use the 'Comfort or Strength' worksheet on Kerboodle to get students to think of different companies that could be named either 'Comfort' or 'Strength'. Ask what goods or services these different companies might offer, and also take the opportunity to introduce the word connotations.

Resources
Kerboodle: 5.5 Comfort or Strength

Picture it

Especially for EAL students, show a picture of a famous company logo. Ask students to tell you the company's name and what the logo suggests to them. Use this activity to discuss the word connotations.

Brand name connotations

Using the 'New brand names' interactive activity on Kerboodle, discuss the list of new brand names and their connotations and then ask students to match them to the products. Note that some may be appropriate for more than one product. Then ask students, working in pairs, to list possible names for an energy bar for athletes that suggest connotations of health and sport. Each pair should vote on their best idea and be ready to feed back to the class with their reasons for the name.

Resources
Kerboodle: 5.5 New brand names

Exploration

Company names

Divide the class into pairs and ask each pair to list ten company names that they are familiar with, before ranking them in order of effectiveness. As a class, discuss the best company names and why they are effective.

High-street names

Before students respond to Activity 1 in the Student Book, you could model how to complete this activity using one of the seven high-street business names in the Student Book, or another suitable business name (not necessarily from the high street).

Resources
Student Book 3: Activity 1, page 118

Who and why?

As a more-detailed exploration of company names, support Activity 1 in the Student Book by asking students to list the names of different companies they know (other than those in the Student Book). They should then complete the 'Who and why?' worksheet on Kerboodle to explain why they think each company chose its name and how it links to its intended target audience.

Resources
Student Book 3: Activity 1, page 118

Kerboodle: 5.5 Who and why?

and guidance

Consolidation

A creative process

The extract from James Caan's autobiography on page 119 of the Student Book provides an insight into a logical – yet creative – way to find a name for a business. It also draws on students' application of cultural context, because it refers to the 1980s (when women were not known to work in the financial sector). Ask students why the word 'Mann' is now outdated and then ask them to consider a new name for Caan's company, with contemporary connotations that take account of a partially female workforce.

Resources

Student Book 3: Activity 2, page 118

Vote

After they have completed Activity 3 in the Student Book, ask students to share their suggested company names and their preferred choice with the rest of their group (including their thinking processes, both in the development and choice of the name). The group should then vote on the best and most appropriate company name to take forward to the final pitch.

Resources

Student Book 3: Activity 3, page 118

Your company name

Caan's naming process is a model for students – researching other company names; thinking of and rejecting ideas; considering the desired connotations of the name; considering how the name will be used; considering the target market; and changing the spelling before coming to a final decision. Students need to follow this process and check their ideas against the bulleted list on page 118 of the Student Book. You could suggest that certain students use the 'Your company name' worksheet on Kerboodle to help them, if necessary. Sharing ideas with another student from their group will also help to develop the thinking process.

Resources

Student Book 3: Activity 3, page 118

Kerboodle: 5.5 Your company name

Metacognition

To develop higher-order thinking, ask volunteers from each group to explain to the class how they came up with their company name. Ask how this exercise could help them when they are choosing words for writing in general.

Ridiculous names?

Use a company name generator (such as the weblink below) to create a number of fictional company names. Ask the class to comment on whether the names generated are appropriate or not – giving reasons for their decisions. Then ask students whether the generated names are better or worse than the ones they came up with for their own companies? Why or why not?

Resources

Weblink: www.panabee.com

The best words

Ask students to rank the following names for a fizzy drink: Dizzy, Guzzle, Taste, Triumph, and Clarity. Choose students to give reasons for their best and worst names.

Extra Time

Ask students to write a short article for other new entrepreneurs, explaining the importance of getting the name right for their new product.

Lesson focus

Why are we teaching this?

Being concise, yet clear, is a skill that most writers need to practise, because it's important but not easy. In this lesson, students will practise and develop this skill through the process of drawing up a brief business plan for their proposed business idea.

What are students learning?

Students will be able to:

- explore techniques to summarize and present information clearly and concisely.

How you could teach this

A variety of activities and approaches are provided on the right for you to select from and adapt to meet the needs of your students. The Kerboodle lesson player sequence is derived from these suggestions, to act as a starting point for your lesson.

Teaching suggestions

Ignition

Cut it out

Ask students to reduce the text of a film review to 15 words, using the 'Cut it out' worksheet on Kerboodle (or another film review of your choice). Explain to the class that this task is practice for writing concisely and clearly later in the lesson.

Resources
Kerboodle: 5.6 Cut it out

Where will you locate?

Ask students, working in pairs from the same group, to respond to Activity 1 in the Student Book by considering the ideal location for their proposed business – with their reasons. Tell them that if they don't need particular premises they should focus on their equipment needs instead.

Resources
Student Book 3: Activity 1, page 120

A concise advert

Write the following sentence on the board: 'I really want a large shop space in central Birmingham to display my brand new product – the Expandable Cycle – very cheaply.' Ask students what words they would cut out and change to make an advert of nine or ten words.

Exploration

Wanted

Support Activities 2a–2c in the Student Book by using the 'Wanted!' worksheet on Kerboodle to support and improve students' writing. Emphasize the importance of punctuation, clarity and a concise choice of words.

Resources
Student Book 3: Activities 2a–2c, page 120

Kerboodle: 5.6 Wanted!

Creative premises

Google is well known for its alternative approach to office space (see the picture gallery on the weblink below). Use the 'Creative premises' worksheet on Kerboodle to encourage students to design a more-creative office space for their own business. Then ask them to write a concise and clear email of no more than 100 words to their company director explaining what they would like and how it would help the business to work well.

Resources
Kerboodle: 5.6 Creative premises

Weblink: http://www.telegraph.co.uk/technology/picture-galleries/9461561/Inside-Googles-quirky-new-London-headquarters.html?frame=2303567

Answers

Answers to Student Book activities, where relevant, can be found on page 129.

and guidance

Consolidation

Summarize

Use the weblinks below to show the class a careers video clip from either Innocent or Google. Ask students to summarize the video clip clearly and concisely, using the following question as a focus: 'Why work for this company?' Then ask each student to swap their summary with a partner and check that their partner's writing is as clear and concise as it could be. Finally they should redraft their own summary, using the feedback from their partner as a guide.

Resources

Weblinks: http://www.innocentdrinks.co.uk/us/careers

http://www.google.co.uk/about/jobs/lifeatgoogle/

Financial planning

Emphasize that students need to carefully follow the instructions in Student Book Activities 3 and 4 in order to produce a financial plan for their proposed business. Explain that they are working towards a clear and concise overview of their finances for the potential investors in their final end-of-unit pitch. Use the 'Example financial plan' presentation on Kerboodle to support these activities, which might be best completed in business groups rather than individually.

Resources

Student Book, Activities 3–4, page 121

Kerboodle: 5.6 Example financial plan

Fact sheet

You could suggest that students design an informative fact sheet (including key financial information, graphs and pie charts) for their final end-of-unit pitch. This would be a good opportunity for students to demonstrate their IT skills. This fact sheet could then be redrafted, if necessary, in a later lesson for use in the final end-of-unit pitch.

Resources

Student Book 3: Activity 4, page 121

Financial mini-pitch

Divide the class into groups consisting of a representative from each of the main business groups, so that each representative can present their group's financial plans to the others. Remind them that when they present their group's plans, they will be acting as the entrepreneur and the other students will be possible investors. After each entrepreneur has presented their plan, each investor should give feedback about whether they would invest in that business or not – with their reasons. The investors should also suggest improvements and costs that the entrepreneur and their group may not have considered.

Lesson summary: Tweet

Ask students to summarize the learning in the lesson in a concise and clear 140-character Tweet. You could simplify this by asking for 10 words instead of 140 characters.

Top tips

Divide the class into pairs and ask students to take turns listing top tips to help their partner reduce a text so that it is clear and concise.

Three-minute diagram

Give students three minutes (or half the time left in the lesson) to draw a diagram or illustration showing the best ways to reduce a text clearly. Ask them to explain their diagram to a partner.

Extra Time

Ask students to write a persuasive formal reply (in the form of an email) to the 'Wanted' advertisement in Activity 2. Remind them to use formal language, but at the same time to make sure that their premises or equipment seem inviting, fitting and flawless to the person advertising.

 Weblink   Presentation   Interactive activity

Lesson focus

Why are we teaching this?

Students need to focus on the presentation of a pitch as well as its content, because most of the meaning in a presentation comes from the non-verbal techniques used. In this lesson, students will have the opportunity to develop their presentation skills through practice and peer assessment.

What are students learning?

Students will be able to:

● explore the use of verbal and non-verbal techniques to promote and sell a product.

How you could teach this

A variety of activities and approaches are provided on the right for you to select from and adapt to meet the needs of your students. The Kerboodle lesson player sequence is derived from these suggestions, to act as a starting point for your lesson.

Teaching suggestions

Ignition

Useful quotes

Before they respond to Activity 1 in the Student Book, ask students to read the three quotations from successful entrepreneurs on page 122. These will help them understand which verbal and non-verbal techniques investors are looking for in a pitch. As a kinaesthetic activity, ask the class to stand as in Bubble 2. What impression does this give of a potential entrepreneur?

Resources
Student Book 3: Activity 1, page 122

Advertising jingles

Ask students to think of and discuss advertising jingles they have heard on TV or radio. As a class, discuss what makes these examples effective.

Kinaesthetic

Tell students to stand as they would when delivering a pitch in front of potential investors. Point out students who seem confident but relaxed in their body language and facial expressions for praise, and use them as models for the rest of the class.

Exploration

Levi Roots image

Show the image from Kerboodle of Levi Roots presenting his pitch to the Dragons' Den. Discuss with the class how the way he dresses and stands, and his facial expression, all add to his personality.

Resources
Kerboodle: 5.7 Levi Roots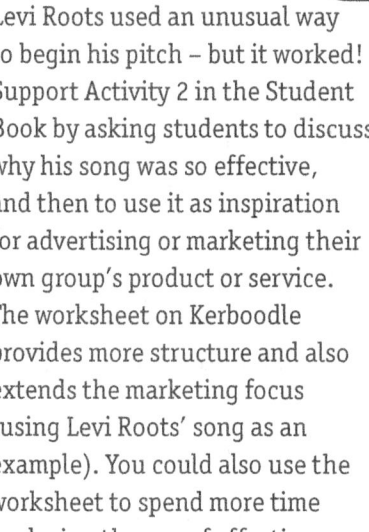

Levi Roots' song

Levi Roots used an unusual way to begin his pitch – but it worked! Support Activity 2 in the Student Book by asking students to discuss why his song was so effective, and then to use it as inspiration for advertising or marketing their own group's product or service. The worksheet on Kerboodle provides more structure and also extends the marketing focus (using Levi Roots' song as an example). You could also use the worksheet to spend more time exploring the use of effective verbal skills.

Resources
Student Book 3: Activity 2, page 122

Kerboodle: 5.7 Verbal skills and marketing

Answers

Answers to Student Book activities, where relevant, can be found on page 129.

and guidance

Consolidation

Ignite English interview

You might like to play Ignite Interview Film 2 to the class, in which Renée Watson discusses reading and writing skills.

Resources
Kerboodle: 5 Ignite Interview Renée Watson Film 2

Levi Roots' pitch

Show Levi Roots' full Dragons' Den appearance from the weblink below. Before they watch the clip, ask students to be prepared to comment on: how he speaks; how he moves; his qualities. After they have made notes, discuss what they can learn from his pitch.

Resources
Weblink: www.leviroots.com/video/

A mini-pitch

As part of their preparation for Activity 3 in the Student Book, suggest that lower-attaining students complete a quick spider-diagram to collect together their ideas before writing the short verbal pitch. You could ask quicker or higher-attaining students to complete the Stretch activity in the Student Book by using the 'Developing a TV advertisement' worksheet on Kerboodle.

Resources
Student Book 3: Activity 3, page 122

Kerboodle: 5.7 Developing a TV advertisement

Visual impact

Think about and share how you can support students in improving the visual impact of their pitch. Can they have access to computers, coloured paper, large pens, props, etc?

Resources
Student Book 3: Activity 4, page 123

Student models

Choose several students to model performing their mini-pitches in front of the class, and praise good practice. Ask for one constructive feedback comment from another student in the class (depending on students' confidence).

Progress Check

Ask students to pair up and present their mini-pitches to each other. Use the 'Persuasive pitch Progress Check' worksheet on Kerboodle to guide their assessment of the verbal and non-verbal techniques being used.

Resources
Student Book 3: 5.7 Persuasive pitch Progress Check, page 123

Kerboodle: Persuasive pitch Progress Check

Family

Ask students to imagine that someone else in their family is going to be presenting a pitch on TV to support their product. What presentational advice would they give them?

Target-setting

Write the following target on the board: 'Show enthusiasm'. Ask students to provide some more detail, so that it's easier to achieve it. For example, speak in an enthusiastic tone of voice and use one or two appropriate hand gestures. Ask them to improve their own targets from the Progress Check activity by making them more specific.

Answer stems

Ask students to come up with five different ways to begin answering a question, while giving them time to think. For example: 'Thank you for that question.' or 'This is a good time to tell you about …'.

Extra Time

Ask students to create a jingle (or catchy song) for an online marketing campaign. It could be played in advertising and when their company's webpage is opened.

Lesson focus

Why are we teaching this?

While the focus in this lesson is on a business pitch and job interviews, students will also be learning the transferable skills of responding to questions with confidence and purpose in a challenging situation.

What are students learning?

Students will be able to:

- develop techniques for effective listening, questioning and responding to others during role-play.

How you could teach this

A variety of activities and approaches are provided on the right for you to select from and adapt to meet the needs of your students. The Kerboodle lesson player sequence is derived from these suggestions, to act as a starting point for your lesson.

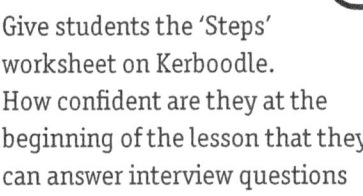

Teaching suggestions

Ignition

If this is the answer ...

Ask students for possible questions about their proposed businesses to go with these answers: (a) £200; (b) Never.

Steps

Give students the 'Steps' worksheet on Kerboodle. How confident are they at the beginning of the lesson that they can answer interview questions successfully? (They will return to this later.)

Resources
Kerboodle: 5.8 Steps

After school

Ask students to list when they think they might have to answer spoken questions in life outside school, e.g. cold callers, in a shop or buying a ticket. Hold a class discussion about which questions are the easiest to answer and why.

Exploration

Reading to learn

After reading the extract in the Student Book, ask students to respond to Activity 1 by thinking about which of the techniques mentioned would also be relevant in an interview situation. However, before they attempt this activity, discuss interviews with students. Have they experienced or seen an interview? What did they learn about them?

Resources
Student Book 3: Activity 1, page 124

Dragons' steps

After reading the Dragons' tips on answering questions, ask students to apply those tips to interviews by imagining that they are interviewing or being interviewed for a job in their proposed business. For support, draw their attention to the example questions. An interview could be role-played by confident students in front of the class as a model.

Resources
Student Book 3: Activities 2a–2d, page 124

Answers

Answers to Student Book activities, where relevant, can be found on page 129.

Key for Kerboodle LRA resources Lesson Player Image Video  Worksheet

and guidance

Question stems

Hand out the 'Question stems' worksheet on Kerboodle and ask students to list all of the words that could begin a question. Then ask them to sort those words into two groups – one for words that begin questions leading to one-word answers (closed), and another for words that begin questions leading to longer answers (open). Then ask which questions they think would be most useful in (a) a pitch, (b) an interview or (c) a multiple-choice quiz.

Resources

Student Book 3: Activity 2b, page 124

Kerboodle: 5.8 Question stems

Interview example

Show the class a video clip of an interview, e.g. from *The Apprentice*. Ask students to make a note of:

- examples of open and closed questions
- what the interviewee does well
- how the interviewee could improve.

Resources

Weblink: www.bbc.co.uk (search using '*The Apprentice* interviews')

Share a winning answer

After the interview role-plays in Activity 2c, ask students to feed back an excellent answer that someone else made. Ask others to say why it was a good answer.

Progress Check and feedback

Ask students to use the 'Interview feedback Progress Check' worksheet on Kerboodle to structure and develop their interview feedback for Activity 2d in more depth.

Resources

Student Book 3: Activity 2d, page 124

Kerboodle: 5.8 Interview feedback Progress Check

Teacher in role

If possible, role-play an excellent and a poor interview with another teacher, or ask students interested in drama to perform. Ask students to 'spot the differences' between the two interviews.

Body language

Model different ways of sitting and ask students to comment on the impressions given out to observers by the different positions. Then ask students to suggest the best way to sit in an interview: (a) when asking questions (b) when answering questions.

Consolidation

Top tips

Ask students to give their five top tips for answering questions during an interview.

Steps

Return to the 'Steps' worksheet given out at the beginning of the lesson. Ask students to think about it again. Has their confidence increased? If not, why not? What is stopping their progress?

Resources

Kerboodle: 5.8 Steps

Extra Time

Ask students watch a clip from *Dragons' Den* and write a short paragraph about the entrepreneur's skill in listening and responding to questions. Encourage them to focus on their strengths and weaknesses.

Lesson focus

Why are we teaching this?

Students analyse a model pitch in order to prepare their own group pitch for the end-of-unit assessment in the following lesson. The model builds on what students have already covered, by demonstrating the use of props, formal language and financial information. This lesson also models and emphasizes the importance of effective planning and preparation – something that students can often rush.

What are students learning?

Students will be able to:

- analyse a successful pitch, noting techniques that are effective and can be used for other pitches
- prepare a pitch using effective planning, drafting and rehearsing techniques.

How you could teach this

A variety of activities and approaches are provided on the right for you to select from and adapt to meet the needs of your students. The Kerboodle lesson player sequence is derived from these suggestions, to act as a starting point for your lesson.

Answers

Answers to Student Book activities, where relevant, can be found on page 129.

Teaching suggestions

Ignition

A successful pitch

Using their prior learning, ask students to discuss what they believe will make a successful pitch, first in pairs, then as a whole class. Using the 'Successful pitch' interactive activity on Kerboodle, ask students to rank the options in order of importance. As a class, discuss the ranking. Draw out that some things may be equally important.

Resources

Kerboodle: 5.9 Successful pitch

Viewed pitches

Ask students to think of pitches they have already seen during this unit, at home online, or on TV. Discuss a successful pitch such as Levi Roots' or another. What made it successful?

Star qualities

Show the image gallery on Kerboodle of some famous entrepreneurs and discuss with students what qualities they seem to have in common. Follow this up by asking students: 'If you had £10,000 to invest, what qualities or skills would you need to see in someone before lending them your money?'

Resources

Kerboodle: 5.9 Famous entrepreneurs

Exploration

Sammy French: A successful pitch

Use Activities 1–4 in the Student Book to encourage students to analyse Sammy French's pitch from *Dragons' Den*, in order to help them prepare their own pitches for the final end-of-unit assessment in the next lesson.

Resources

Student Book 3: Activities 1–4, page 126

Structure

Analysing the structure of Sammy's pitch will help students to decide what to include in their own pitches and how to order them. Use cards made from the Kerboodle worksheet to make this activity more kinaesthetic.

Resources

Student Book 3: Activity 3, page 126

Kerboodle: 5.9 Reorder on cards

Ignite English interview

You might like to play Ignite Interview Film 1 to the class. In this film we are introduced to Renée Watson and her thoughts about creating a business.

Resources

Kerboodle: 5 Ignite Interview Renée Watson Film 1

and guidance

Consolidation

Fit Fur Life name

Remind students that the choice of words and language is important in a name, by asking them to analyse the name that Sammy French gave her business. As support, ask them what devices are used in the name Fit Fur Life. What does the alliteration and deliberate misspelling add? What does it tell them about the product?

Resources
Student Book 3: Activity 4, page 126

Preparing the pitch

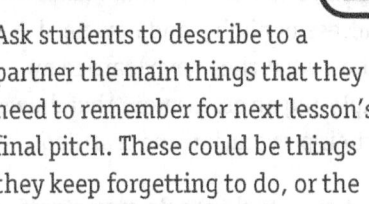

Take students through the process of preparing their final end-of-unit group pitches on pages 128–129 of the Student Book. Consider what resources you can offer them: large sheets of paper, computer and printer access, sticky notes, coloured paper, pens, etc. They will need note cards in the final stages of preparation.

Make sure that each student in the group has been given a suitable area of the pitch to present, so that they have sufficient opportunity to demonstrate their spoken English skills. When drafting, encourage them to read the pitch aloud to check, change and correct it. When rehearsing, they will need to work in pairs to assess each other.

Preparation

Ask students, without looking at the Student Book, to describe the preparation stages for a pitch or speech. This will reinforce the importance of preparation and planning.

Teacher to model

Model how you would prepare a pitch. Show students different ways of making notes: spider diagram, notes, cards, symbols. Remind students that they need to take their ideas and organize them into the most useful and logical order.

Self assessment

As well as peer assessing, you could also suggest that students use the 'Pitch self-assessment checklist' on Kerboodle to ensure that they are on track and also to decide what they need to improve before the actual assessment next lesson.

Resources
Kerboodle: 5.9 Pitch self-assessment checklist

Summarize

Ask students to describe to a partner the main things that they need to remember for next lesson's final pitch. These could be things they keep forgetting to do, or the main points of their part of the presentation.

What's the best idea?

Ask students to share something good they heard this lesson, something encouraging or just a good idea. This will help them to feel confident about the final assessment.

Be positive

Encourage students in each group to boost each other's confidence in preparation for the final assessment. Ask them to tell a partner at least two things they have done well in their preparation.

Extra Time

Ask students to watch a successful pitch from a show such as *The Apprentice*. They should note down what they think made it successful and try to incorporate some of these aspects into their own pitch.

Assessment focus

Why are we assessing this?

Students have completed a unit on how to prepare a business pitch (at the same time as developing reading, speaking, listening, and formal writing skills). They have considered what makes a successful pitch – and now need to show what they have learned by completing an assessment that draws on their preparation and learning.

What are students demonstrating?

Students will be able to:

- present a formal business pitch with confidence and enthusiasm, using the planning, drafting and rehearsal from the previous lesson.

How to deliver the assessment

Suggestions and guidance on how to set up and prepare your students for the assessment are provided, as well as possible approaches to marking the assessment.

Alternative/additional assessment

There is an alternative end-of-unit assessment available on Kerboodle. This assessment leads to a written outcome and can be used either in addition to or instead of the Student Book end-of-unit assessment.

Resources

Kerboodle: 5.10 Alternative end-of-unit assessment 📄

Assessment suggestions and guidance

Understanding the assessment

Check that students understand the assessment task. Emphasize that they are being assessed on their spoken English skills.

Although they actually prepared and rehearsed their pitches last lesson, students will need at least five minutes to go through their notes and refresh their memories. Also check that they have all props and equipment they need.

You could invite a senior leader, visitors from local businesses and/or the head of department to act as one of the two potential investors. At the end of the lesson, give feedback on which group's business pitch has been chosen to receive the investment – with the investors' reasons.

Resources

Student Book 3: pages 130–131

Timing expectations

If you are concerned that some presentations might be too long, you could time them. For example, you could use a stopwatch to ensure that each group's pitch is no longer than seven or eight minutes (with three extra minutes for questions). Warn students about these time limits and say that the potential investors will be in charge and will have the power to stop the pitch once the agreed time limit has been reached.

Marking

You will want to mark this in line with departmental and school marking guidelines. If you wish, you could use the Ignite English marking scales provided on Kerboodle. Using the Ignite English marking scales will help you to identify specific strengths and areas for improvement.

Refer to the KS3 National Curriculum and Ignite English mapping grids on pages 154–156 of this Teacher Companion to identify other Ignite English units where these spoken English skills are covered, or ask students to use the SPAG interactives on Kerboodle to address any areas identified for improvement. The Grammar Reference Guide on Kerboodle contains definitions and additional examples of each of the spelling, punctuation and grammar points covered in the interactives, for your reference.

Resources

Kerboodle: 5 Ignite English marking scales 📄

Kerboodle: SPAG interactives 🖱

Kerboodle: Grammar Reference Guide

Student Book answers

Below are the answers to any largely non-subjective Student Book activities contained within this unit.

Lesson 4

1 Informal words, phrases and abbreviations:
- 'best bet'
- 'he would get say 17sh.'
- 'save us the **odd** 10sh'

Incomplete sentences:
- [There are] 'So few days now until the holidays.'

Informal question to end:
- 'How about it?'

Lesson 8

1 All of the techniques could be applied to an interview situation.

Lesson 9

1 Sammy proves that her product works using evidence and figures proving that there is a large target market. Students should use an example from paragraph one of Sammy's pitch to prove this.

2 She uses figures to prove that she has already sold '147 units' and needs to produce more to meet demand. Students could use evidence from paragraph 2 of Sammy's pitch to prove this.

3 Order: c, a, d and b

Unit 6: From Talking Drums to Tweets

Unit overview

Why are we teaching this?

This unit allows students to explore ways in which changes in communications technology have influenced language – investigating the **influence of modern technologies**, such as smartphones and social media, as well as how technologies such as African talking drums and the introduction of the printing press have affected **language change**.

It enables students to develop their **analytical skills as readers**, as well as providing opportunities for them to practise **discussion**, **interviewing** and **presentational skills**. The core skills of **communication and literacy in oral and written contexts** lie at the heart of this unit, with the exploration of these in a range of contexts allowing students to reflect upon their own language use.

What are the learning aims?

By the end of the unit, students will be able to:

- comment on how different forms of communications technology influence the ways in which language is used
- analyse and respond to different viewpoints and present their own views on an issue
- adapt phrases, sentence structures and conventions to communicate the same information through different media
- communicate information and ideas clearly – selecting an appropriate tone, pace and intonation, and structuring their talk effectively.

How will this be assessed?

Key assessment task	Focus for assessment
Student Book: Giving a presentation about modern communications technology and language change.	<ul><li>Communicating information and ideas clearly.</li><li>Selecting an appropriate tone, pace and intonation.</li><li>Structuring talk effectively, drawing on research and own experiences to illustrate key points.</li></ul>
Kerboodle: Writing an article for a website for parents about the impact of new technology on teenagers.	<ul><li>Creating an appropriate tone, using Standard English and drawing on rhetorical devices for persuasive effect.</li><li>Structuring the article effectively, using cohesive devices, and also supporting ideas and arguments with factual detail.</li><li>Using a range of vocabulary, sentence structures and punctuation precisely.</li></ul>

The end-of-unit assessment on Kerboodle can be used either instead of or in addition to the Student Book end-of-unit assessment.

Note that short Progress Checks also feature in this unit, providing formative assessment opportunities to support the students' learning.

Lesson sequence

This is a suggested lesson sequence, but you might choose to alter or add to it to suit your particular teaching needs.

Introducing the unit

1 Communication Breakdown

- Activate students' prior knowledge about communications technology.
- Respond to the Ignite interview featuring Fiona McPherson.
- Analyse and respond to different viewpoints and present personal views on an issue.
- Read a newspaper article exploring the negative impacts of modern communications technology.
- Discuss and devise rules for the correct use of modern communications technology.

---

2 Smart Phones?	3 Talking Drums	4 Twitter and Telegrams
• Consider and discuss views about the positive and negative effects of technological change. • Read a newspaper article about the results of a survey on the impact of modern technology on young people. • Consider the skills required in the modern workplace and present views on how modern technology can affect them.	• Explore how different forms of communications technology influence the way language is used. • Read an extract from *The Information* by James Gleick. • Write 'talking drum' phrases, providing clarifying information to make the meaning clear.	• Explore how different forms of communications technology influence the way language is used. • Adapt phrases, sentence structures and conventions to communicate the same information in different media. • Read a blog post exploring the similarities between Twitter and the telegram.
5 The Printed Word	**6 From A to Squee!**	**7 Telephone Tone**
• Consider the role of the printing press in the development of the English language. • Read and analyse an extract from *The Canterbury Tales* by Geoffrey Chaucer. • Explore differences between Middle English and Modern English.	• Investigate the role of the dictionary in the development of the English language. • Explore how vocabulary develops and changes over time. • Read extracts from early English dictionaries and a blog post from Oxford Dictionaries Online about new vocabulary.	• Use inflection and intonation to actively involve a listener and communicate meaning. • Understand how to move between formal and informal registers in different contexts. • Role-play a phone call to complain about mobile phone service.
8 Live News	**9 Digital Generations**	**10 Assessment**
• Compare the language and structure of live blogging with newspaper reports. • Read an extract from a live blog reporting on the birth of the Duke and Duchess of Cambridge's baby and a newspaper report on the same event. • Discuss the advantages and disadvantages of each form.	• Explore the ways in which different generations use technology to enable communication. • Read a newspaper article presenting interviews with three generations of the same family. • Interview others about communications technology usage.	• Student Book: Give a presentation about modern communications technology and language change. • Kerboodle: Writing an article for a website for parents about the impact of new technology on teenagers.

Preparing to teach

Refresh your knowledge

You might find it helpful to refer to the following key points when planning your teaching of this unit.

- The evolution of communications technology began thousands of years ago, in prehistory, with drums and smoke signals being used to communicate information over distances in Africa, America and parts of Asia.

- Johannes Gutenberg introduced movable type printing to Europe in around 1439. This system of printing used movable pieces of metal type and enabled the mass production of books. William Caxton introduced the printing press to England in the second half of the 15th century, and printed the majority of his books in the English language. These developments heralded the era of mass communication – leading to sharp increases in literacy levels and the spreading of information and ideas across the planet.

- King Charles I opened the use of his own mail service (the 'royal mail') to the public in 1635, and the General Post Office was established in 1657. However, the postal system at this time was both expensive and complex (with the cost of postage being worked out according to the distance a letter was being sent and the number of sheets of paper it contained). It was only in 1840 that the current system of uniform postage, charged by weight, was introduced nationwide.

- Before the widespread use of telephones (and latterly the Internet) for communication, telegrams were used to send messages across great distances. In 1913, over 82 million telegrams were sent in the UK. Telegrams reached their greatest popularity in the period up to the Second World War. The convention of using the word 'STOP' to end sentences (in place of a full stop), became peculiar to the telegram because the inclusion of this four-letter word was free, whereas punctuation incurred an extra charge!

Links and further reading

- The following BBC news article explains how the Internet is changing language: www.bbc.co.uk/news/technology-10971949

- Below is a comprehensive article about language and technology from the late Andrew Moore's Universal Teacher website: www.universalteacher.org.uk/lang/languageandtechnology.htm

- An infographic about the evolution of communication can be found at: www.viralblog.com/wp-content/uploads/2013/03/Evolution-of-Communication-Infographic.jpg

Please note that OUP is not responsible for third-party content. Although all links were correct at the time of publication, the content and location of this material may change.

Planning guidance and teaching tips

Think about how you can make the materials relevant to your students and responsive to their needs. Some suggested approaches to address key areas are provided below.

- To support their speaking skills throughout the course of the unit, be prepared to work with students who are **less confident about their use of spoken English**, especially EAL students, in **one-to-one and guided group contexts**. Consider which strategies you could use to keep their interest and build their confidence, e.g. clearly defining their role in discussions and **providing clear models of Standard English** to follow.

- Give students space to **speak from the position of experts** when discussing the communications technology they use. Creating opportunities for students to see the value of the knowledge they bring into the classroom can help to motivate them, and also enable them to challenge expectations in terms of their level of attainment.

- Think about the range of **communications technology** that you have available in your department, and how you could make use of it to support the Student Book and Teacher Companion activities. For example, you could allow students access to micro-blogging tools to support the live blogging activity in Lesson 8.

- Try to provide opportunities for students to speak to and work with **individuals who use communications technology** as part of their working lives, in order to emphasize the relevance and importance of this unit in the real world.

Lesson focus

Why are we teaching this?

Lesson 1 launches this unit by providing students with the opportunity to reflect on their own use of communications technology, as well as sharing their own views – and evaluating the views of others – about the positive and negative effects of mobile phones, laptops and social media.

What are students learning?

Students will be able to:

- analyse and respond to different viewpoints and present their own views on an issue.

How you could teach this

A variety of activities and approaches are provided on the right for you to select from and adapt to meet the needs of your students. The Kerboodle lesson player sequence is derived from these suggestions, to act as a starting point for your lesson.

Teaching suggestions

Ignition

Ignite English interview

You might like to play Ignite Interview Film 1 to the class. In this film we are introduced to Fiona McPherson, Oxford English Dictionary Editor, and her thoughts about language change.

Resources

Kerboodle: 6 Ignite Interview Fiona McPherson Film 1

Technology audit

Working in pairs, ask students to list the different types of technology they have used to communicate in the past week, e.g. mobile phone, laptop, landline telephone, etc. Now ask students to list the different ways in which they have read for information or for pleasure in the past week, e.g. reading online news websites, reading an e-reader, reading a printed text, etc. Create a list of communications technology used by the class and discuss how this has changed over time.

Resources

Student Book 3: Activities 1 and 2, page 133

A world without technology

Ask students to imagine a world in which there are no phones, no computers and no modern forms of communications technology! Discuss what it would be like to live in such a world – how would it affect the ways in which people work, live and are educated?

Exploration

Shared reading

Use shared reading of the newspaper article on page 135 of the Student Book to identify the negative effects ascribed to the use of phones, laptops and social media on modern manners, e.g. 'constant use of mobile phones and social media in the office', 'the written skills of young employees were "appalling"', 'a rift between virtual and real world personalities', etc. Highlight how the article embeds quotations from the survey.

Resources

Student Book 3: Activity 1, page 134

Counter-arguments

Use the 'Counter-arguments' worksheet on Kerboodle to help students develop arguments that present the positive benefits of communications technology on people's manners.

Resources

Student Book 3: Activity 2, page 134

Kerboodle: 6.1 Counter-arguments

Answers

Answers to Student Book activities, where relevant, can be found on page 153.

and guidance

Role-play

Ask students to work in pairs to role-play an encounter between a customer and a shop assistant, where the shop assistant is constantly being distracted by their smartphone. Discuss how frustrated the customer might feel at the constant interruptions to their conversation, and how this frustration might be expressed.

Class discussion

You could address Activities 2 and 3 in the Student Book by holding an overall class discussion. Ask students to suggest some ways in which modern communications technology might have improved people's manners, e.g. being able to text a friend to let them know that you are going to be late, etc. Now ask them to suggest some ways in which modern communications technology has made people ruder, e.g. people looking at their mobile and not at the person talking to them, etc. Encourage students to draw on examples from their own lives. Take a class vote on whether mobile phones, laptops and social media have made people more or less polite.

Resources
Student Book 3: Activities 2 and 3, page 134

Mobile etiquette

You could build on and support Activity 4 in the Student Book by asking students to define the word 'etiquette' (to check their understanding). Then use the weblink below to display and discuss a *Telegraph* article that provides Debrett's ten rules for mobile phone etiquette. Ask students to say whether they disagree with any of the ten rules – with their reasons.

Resources
Student Book 3: Activity 4, page 134

Weblink: http://www.telegraph.co.uk/technology/8679038/Debretts-guide-to-mobile-phone-etiquette.html

Writing rules

Support Activity 4 in the Student Book by using the 'Writing rules' worksheet on Kerboodle to revise the conventions of instructional writing. Encourage students to consider the audience for their etiquette guide, e.g. teenagers, older mobile phone users, etc., and discuss how this will influence their language choices.

Resources
Student Book 3: Activity 4, page 134

Kerboodle: 6.1 Writing rules

Consolidation

Evaluation

Ask students to swap the set of rules they created in response to Activity 4 in the Student Book with a partner. Encourage them to provide ratings for the appropriateness of their partner's rules, and also how effectively they have been expressed.

Etiquette role-play

Ask students, working in small groups, to create role-plays that show their etiquette rules from Activity 4 in action. You could suggest that they role-play the same situation twice – firstly demonstrating how not to use a mobile phone in a social situation, and then showing someone following their etiquette rules.

Extra Time

Ask students to keep a diary monitoring their use of mobile phones, laptops and social media for a week.

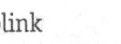

Lesson focus

Why are we teaching this?

This lesson provides students with an opportunity to consider further views about the positive and negative effects of technological change. Students will evaluate some survey results, before reflecting on the skills required in the modern workplace and how these could be improved or negatively affected by technology. Placing the discussion in the context of students' future careers can aid motivation and enhance the relevance of the activities that students undertake.

What are students learning?

Students will be able to:

● consider and discuss views about the positive and negative effects of technological change.

How you could teach this

A variety of activities and approaches are provided on the right for you to select from and adapt to meet the needs of your students. The Kerboodle lesson player sequence is derived from these suggestions, to act as a starting point for your lesson.

Answers

Answers to Student Book activities, where relevant, can be found on page 153.

Teaching suggestions

Ignition

Dumb technology

Display the question: 'Is technology making us stupid?' Take a class vote and ask students to justify the answer they give.

Mobile minds

Use the weblink below to show the video exploring the different features of the Samsung Galaxy Note 3 (or find a similar video online). Discuss the ways in which the phone's benefits are being presented. Then ask students to discuss which of the phone's features they think could be used to improve their knowledge and intelligence.

Resources
Weblink: www.samsung.com/uk/discover/mobile/samsung-galaxy-note-3-and-galaxy-gear-the-perfect-match/

Future smartphones

Using the 'Smartphones' interactive activity on Kerboodle, ask students to rank the uses of a smartphone. Then, based on their discussion, ask students to design a smartphone of the future – with features and apps designed to maximize the user's skills and intelligence. After students have fed back their suggestions, ask the class to vote for those features they think would be the most useful.

Resources
Kerboodle: 6.2 Smartphones

Exploration

Shared reading

Use shared reading of the newspaper article on page 136 of the Student Book to identify how the writer presents the results of the survey in a balanced way, e.g. an introductory paragraph presenting both viewpoints, describing the results of the survey as 'fairly evenly split', alternating between paragraphs presenting positive and negative views about the effects of technology, etc. Discuss how these techniques can also be used in spoken contexts, such as presentations and debates.

Statements

Use the 'Statements' worksheet on Kerboodle to extend Activity 1 in the Student Book. Encourage students to give examples from their own lives to support the statements they agree with.

Resources
Student Book 3: Activity 1, page 137

Kerboodle: 6.2 Statements

and guidance

Research and presentation

You could support Activity 2 in the Student Book by asking students to use the weblink below, and other resources, to carry out further research into the results of the survey mentioned in the Student Book article. (The weblink provides the original information on which the article was based.) Then ask them to use their research to create a presentation giving their personal views about whether technology makes people more or less intelligent.

Resources

Student Book 3: Activity 2, page 137

Weblink: www.pewinternet.org/ Reports/2012/Hyperconnected- lives/Overview.aspx

Employment skills

Ask students to use the 'Employment skills' interactive activity on Kerboodle to identify how technology could be used to support different skills in the workplace.

Resources

Student Book 3: Activities 3a and 3b, page 137

Kerboodle: 6.2 Employment skills

Workplace of the future

Elicit from students the future jobs and careers they are interested in. Then ask them to discuss how new technology could affect these careers in the future. Emphasize that they should consider how existing skills might change, and also which new skills might be required. Use the 'Workplace of the future' worksheet on Kerboodle to support this activity.

Resources

Student Book 3: Activities 3a, 3b and 4, page 137

Kerboodle: 6.2 Workplace of the future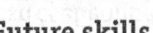

Model writing

Model writing the opening of an email to the CBI in response to Activity 4 in the Student Book. Discuss your choice of subject line and salutation, and highlight the language choices you are making to create an appropriately formal tone.

Resources

Student Book 3: Activity 4, page 137

Progress Check

Ask students, working in pairs, to assess each other's writing in response to Activity 4 in the Student Book. Encourage them to use the 'Progress Check' worksheet on Kerboodle to support this evaluation.

Resources

Kerboodle: 6.2 Progress Check

Future skills

Ask students to discuss and vote for the most important skills they think young people will need in the workplace of the future. Use the list of skills on page 137 of the Student Book as the starting point, and encourage students to suggest any new skills which they think will be important.

Clever tech

Reprise the Ignition activity by displaying the question: 'Is technology making us stupid?' again. Take a new class vote and ask students to justify the answers they give. Discuss whether any students have changed their views and why.

Extra Time

Ask students to interview their friends and family to find out whether they think technological change is making people more or less intelligent.

Lesson focus

Why are we teaching this?

This lesson will enable students to consider one of the oldest forms of communications technology – African talking drums – and to explore the influence this technology had on the way language was used. After reading an extract from James Gleick's *The Information*, students will have the opportunity to experiment with language to explore the connections between content and expression.

What are students learning?

Students will be able to:

● explore how different forms of communications technology influence the way language is used.

How you could teach this

A variety of activities and approaches are provided on the right for you to select from and adapt to meet the needs of your students. The Kerboodle lesson player sequence is derived from these suggestions, to act as a starting point for your lesson.

Answers

Answers to Student Book activities, where relevant, can be found on page 153.

Teaching suggestions

Ignition

Communication timeline

Use the 'Communication timeline' presentation on Kerboodle, or the weblink below, to discuss the evolution of communications technology.

Resources

Kerboodle: 6.3 Communication timeline

Weblink: www.viralblog.com/wp-content/uploads/2013/03/Evolution-of-Communication-Infographic.jpg

Morse code messages

Use the weblink below to play the Morse code message for S.O.S. Ask students if they can identify the message being sent and the method by which it is being sent. Discuss the advantages and disadvantages of this form of communication.

Resources
Weblink: www.soundsnap.com/tags/morse_code

Message race

Ask students to decide which of the following forms of communications technology could send a message the fastest: carrier pigeons, drums, smoke signals. Discuss students' choices and explain that African talking drums could transmit information at up to 100 mph.

Exploration

Talking drums

Support Activity 1 in the Student Book by using the weblink below to show a video clip of a message being sent using African talking drums. Refer to the teaching text on page 138 of the Student Book to ensure that students understand how the talking drums use high and low-pitched notes to communicate meaning. Discuss the possible advantages and disadvantages of this form of communication.

Resources
Student Book 3: Activity 1, page 139

Weblink: www.youtube.com/watch?v=9dHzlPFUA1E

Talking drum phrases

Use the 'Talking drum phrases' worksheet on Kerboodle to support students when completing Activity 2 in the Student Book. Encourage the use of dictionaries and thesauruses to develop students' vocabulary.

Resources
Student Book 3: Activity 2, page 139

Kerboodle: 6.3 Talking drum phrases

Key for Kerboodle LRA resources Lesson Player Image Video  Worksheet

and guidance

Consolidation

Content/meaning

Using the weblink below, ask students to work out what the text says. Discuss the clues that allowed them to elicit the meaning. Then ask them to write a sentence where the letter order of words has been jumbled up, and to see if their partner can work out the meaning.

Resources

Student Book 3: Activities 3a and 3b, page 139

Weblink: http://playingintheworldgame.files.wordpress.com/2012/09/power.jpg

Homophones and homographs

Use the worksheet on Kerboodle to revise homophones and homographs. Discuss how context helps to clarify meaning – drawing out similarities with the language of the talking drums.

Resources

Kerboodle: 6.3 Homophones and homographs

Discussion

Explain to students which different purposes talking drums have historically been used for. For example: as memory devices for sharing stories about important events and people; to communicate messages across long distances; during celebrations, rituals and ceremonies; to bring people together and help settle disputes. Discuss which modern technologies could be used for each of these purposes.

Encryption

Discuss the problems of long-distance communication using talking drums, e.g. a communication detailing an army's battle plans being overheard by the enemy. Challenge higher-attaining students to suggest possible strategies for encrypting talking drum messages (to ensure that they can be understood by their intended recipient but kept secret from others).

Progress Check

Ask students to create a set of instructions for a simple task where selected letters are omitted from words. Students should swap their instructions and discuss how easy they found them to follow.

Chinese whispers

Give one student a simple message to pass orally around the class. Ask each student passing the message on to add a clarifying phrase to make the meaning of the message even clearer. Ask the last person in the class to share the message they have been given. Discuss how the message has changed.

Checklist

Ask students to create a checklist of advice explaining how to use talking drums to communicate effectively.

Extra Time

Ask students to research other methods of long-distance communication used before the invention of the telephone.

Lesson focus

Why are we teaching this?

In this lesson, students will study a blog post exploring the similarities between Twitter and the telegram. They will investigate how these different forms of communications technology influence the way in which language is used. They will also have the opportunity to practise their editing skills as they adapt vocabulary and sentence structures to communicate the same information using different media.

What are students learning?

Students will be able to:

- explore how different forms of communications technology influence the way language is used
- adapt phrases, sentence structures and conventions to communicate the same information in different media.

How you could teach this

A variety of activities and approaches are provided on the right for you to select from and adapt to meet the needs of your students. The Kerboodle lesson player sequence is derived from these suggestions, to act as a starting point for your lesson.

Answers

Answers to Student Book activities, where relevant, can be found on page 153.

Teaching suggestions

Ignition

Activating prior knowledge

Ask students if they use Twitter. Discuss reasons why people use Twitter and elicit the features of the social network, e.g. 140-character limit for every tweet, use of hashtags, etc.

The price of communication

Select a topical news story and challenge students to summarize it in a single sentence. But explain that they will be charged £1 for every word they use, so they must summarize the story using the fewest number of words possible – whilst still making sure that it can be understood. Ask students to share their messages and discuss the choices they made.

The birth of telecommunications

Use the weblink below to show the class a video about the invention of the telegraph. Discuss how this invention changed society, e.g. allowing information to be communicated over great distances at high speed; changing the physical landscape, with the erection of telegraph poles and wires, etc.

Resources
Weblink: www.history.com/topics/telegraph/videos#the-telegraph-and-telephone

Exploration

Telegrams to tweets

Use the 'Telegrams to tweets' worksheet on Kerboodle to challenge students to report news of famous events as tweets. Then explain that Twitter is used to provide real-time reporting of events (livetweeting), and explore how this could affect writing style, choice of tense, etc. You could share some tweets from Twitter accounts that 'livetweet' historical events, such as @RealTimeWWII (see below).

Resources
Kerboodle: 6.4 Telegrams to tweets

Weblink: https://twitter.com/RealTimeWWII

To catch a murderer

Use the weblink below to introduce the story of how the murderer John Tawell was caught with the aid of a telegram. Ask students to suggest how different forms of communications technology would be used by the police to help solve this case today, e.g. emailing photofit and description of suspect to London police stations, use of Twitter to alert the general public, etc.

Resources
Weblink: www.btp.police.uk/about_us/our_history/crime_history/murder_of_sarah_hart_1845.aspx

  Lesson Player Image Video  Worksheet

and guidance

Shared reading

Ask students to define the word 'brevity'. Use shared reading of the blog post on page 141 of the Student Book to identify the similarities between Twitter and the telegram, and the techniques used to communicate information concisely.

Resources
Student Book 3: Activities 1 and 2, page 140

Twitter tips

You could challenge higher-attaining students to complete Activity 2 in the Student Book by presenting their tips in the form of tweets, using the hashtag #twittertips. Extend the activity by asking students to suggest general tips about how to tweet effectively, e.g. make your tweets informative, useful or interesting to read, etc.

Resources
Student Book 3: Activity 2, page 140

Ignite English interview

You might like to play Ignite Interview Film 1 to the class. In this film we are introduced to Fiona McPherson and her thoughts about language change.

Resources
Kerboodle: 6 Ignite Interview Fiona McPherson Film 1

Editing skills

Use the 'Editing skills' worksheet on Kerboodle to support students when completing Activities 3a and 3b in the Student Book. Encourage them to identify the key points in the text they are editing and discard any unnecessary information.

Resources
Student Book 3: Activities 3a and 3b, page 140

Kerboodle: 6.4 Editing skills

Changing forms

You could support Activity 4 in the Student Book by asking students to write about an upcoming school event, such as a performance of a school play. Divide the class into three groups: ask the first group to write about the event in text-message form; ask the second group to write an email about the event; and ask the third group to write a blog about the event. Share examples from each group and discuss the language choices made in each form.

Resources
Student Book 3: Activity 4, page 140

Consolidation

Evaluation

Ask students to use the twitter tips checklists they created in response to Activity 2b in the Student Book to evaluate each other's responses to Activity 3a. Encourage students to discuss the language choices they made.

Resources
Student Book 3: Activity 3b, page 140

Twitter summary

Ask students to summarize what they have learned in this lesson in a single 140-character tweet.

Communication choices

Ask students to suggest situations where they would use the following forms of communication: Twitter, text message, email, blog, and letter. Discuss students' suggestions and reflect on what their choices suggest about the perceptions of each form.

Extra Time

Ask students to research the history of Twitter.

Lesson focus

Why are we teaching this?

This lesson will give students the opportunity to explore the role of the printing press in the development of the English language – generating a personal response to an extract from William Chaucer's *The Canterbury Tales*, and discussing the implications of the shift to a written culture where the development of a standard form of English begins to emerge.

What are students learning?

Students will be able to:

- consider the role of the printing press in the development of the English language.

How you could teach this

A variety of activities and approaches are provided on the right for you to select from and adapt to meet the needs of your students. The Kerboodle lesson player sequence is derived from these suggestions, to act as a starting point for your lesson.

Answers

Answers to Student Book activities, where relevant, can be found on page 153.

Teaching suggestions

Ignition

Does spelling matter?

Show a deliberately misspelled sentence on the board, e.g. 'I knoww wat you ar thinkin'. Ask students to explain how easy it was for them to work out what the sentence is trying to say. Use this activity as a springboard for a discussion about whether spelling matters.

Pronunciation

Use the weblink below to play some audio files from 'The Prologue' of *The Canterbury Tales*. Ask students to identify the language being spoken and then use the 'Middle English pronunciation' worksheet on Kerboodle to explore pronunciation differences between Middle English and Modern English.

Resources

Weblink: www.nativlang.com/middle-english/middle-english-canterbury-tales.php

Student Book 3: Activities 1–3, page 143

Kerboodle: 6.5 Middle English pronunciation

A world before books

Ask students to imagine a world before books were readily available. Discuss how people would find out information, share ideas, etc.

Exploration

Reading the extract

Ask students, working in pairs, to respond to Activity 1 in the Student Book by reading aloud the extract from *The Canterbury Tales*. Encourage the pairs to use a range of strategies to work out the word meanings, such as phonics and context skills. Remind them that they don't need to translate every word – just work out the overall meaning of the text.

Resources

Student Book 3: Activity 1, page 143

Middle English

Use the 'Middle English' presentation on Kerboodle to follow up Activities 1–3 in the Student Book, by asking students to discuss the linguistic and historical context of Middle English.

Resources

Student Book 3: Activities 1–3, page 143

Kerboodle: 6.5 Middle English

and guidance

Middle English/Modern English

Ask students to work in small groups to discuss the differences they have noticed between Middle English and Modern English. Encourage them to refer to vocabulary from *The Canterbury Tales* extract in the Student Book to support their points.

Resources

Student Book 3: Activity 3, page 143

Timeline

Use the weblink below to display the British Library's interactive timeline to explore the evolution of English language and literature. Highlight the first text in Middle English (1150), the work of medieval illuminators (1240), Chaucer's *The Canterbury Tales* (1400), the Gutenberg Bible (1450), the first English printed book and Caxton's Chaucer (both 1470). Students could conduct this as an independent research activity, if you assign specific key events on the timeline to individual students or student pairs.

Resources

Weblink: www.bl.uk/learning/langlit/evolvingenglish/accessvers/index.html#

Dialects

As a prompt for the discussion of Activity 4 in the Student Book, you could use the weblink below to show the animation exploring dialects and the evolution of a standardized version of English in the Middle Ages.

Resources

Student Book 3: Activity 4, page 143

Weblink: www.bbc.co.uk/learningzone/clips/dialects/6502.html

Consolidation

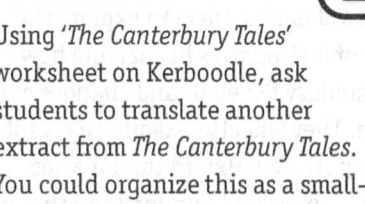

Translations

Using '*The Canterbury Tales*' worksheet on Kerboodle, ask students to translate another extract from *The Canterbury Tales*. You could organize this as a small-group activity – assigning one extract to each group of students.

Resources

Kerboodle: 6.5 *The Canterbury Tales*

Performance

Ask students to work in pairs to perform a reading of *The Canterbury Tales* extract in the Student Book. One student could read the original extract, whilst another student could translate what the first student says into Modern English.

Books forever?

Ask students whether they think books are still needed today in the age of the Internet. Discuss this topic, encouraging students to suggest arguments for and against the continued existence of books.

Extra Time

Ask students to write a short article for the school newspaper that discusses how the creation of books has changed over time.

Lesson focus

Why are we teaching this?

In this lesson, students will have the opportunity to read extracts from two early English dictionaries (*A Table Alphabeticall* and Samuel Johnson's *A Dictionary of the English Language*). This will enable them to explore the role of dictionaries in charting how vocabulary develops and changes over time. They will also examine a recent blog post from Oxford Dictionaries Online, in order to understand that new words are constantly being added to the English language.

What are students learning?

Students will be able to:

- investigate the role of the dictionary in the development of the English language
- explore how vocabulary develops and changes over time.

How you could teach this

A variety of activities and approaches are provided on the right for you to select from and adapt to meet the needs of your students. The Kerboodle lesson player sequence is derived from these suggestions, to act as a starting point for your lesson.

> **Answers**
>
> Answers to Student Book activities, where relevant, can be found on page 153.

Teaching suggestions

Ignition

Definitions

Ask students to provide definitions for the following terms: 'squee', 'buzzworthy', 'omnishambles', 'me time', 'prepping'. As well as providing a definition for each term, ask them to use the word or phrase in context.

Definition matcher

Use the 'Definition matcher' interactive activity on Kerboodle to allow students to match the words from the extract from *A Table Alphabeticall* in the Student Book with the correct definitions.

Resources
Kerboodle: 6.6 Definition matcher

Dictionaries

Ask students to discuss the contexts in which they use dictionaries, e.g. when reading a text to work out the meaning of new vocabulary, checking spelling when writing, etc. Discuss what types of dictionaries students use and why, e.g. online dictionaries, dictionary apps, dictionaries in book form.

Exploration

Shared reading

Use shared reading of the blog post from Oxford Dictionaries Online on page 145 of the Student Book to identify some of the influences behind the new vocabulary included in the dictionary, e.g. fashion and technology. Ask students to suggest some other recently coined words and discuss the influences behind them.

Resources
Student Book 3: Activities 1a and 1b, page 144

Portmanteau words

Use the weblink below, or other online portmanteau word generators, to support students when completing Activities 3a and 3b in the Student Book. Ask students to provide definitions for the best examples they create.

Resources
Student Book 3: Activities 3a and 3b, page 144

Weblink: http://portmanteaur.com/

Ignite English interview

You might like to play Ignite Interview Film 1 to the class. In this film we are introduced to Fiona McPherson and her thoughts about language change.

Resources
Kerboodle: 6 Ignite Interview Fiona McPherson Film 1

and guidance

Consolidation

Britishisms in the USA

Use the weblink below to read and discuss a BBC article that explores how British terms and vocabulary are crossing the Atlantic into American English – so it's not all one-way traffic! Highlight the influences on this trend, such as literature, TV programmes and the Internet.

Resources

Weblink: www.bbc.co.uk/news/magazine-19670686

Word origins

As an introduction to Activity 5 in the Student Book, use the 'Word origins' presentation on Kerboodle to explore English words that have come from other languages.

Resources

Student Book 3: Activity 5, page 146

Kerboodle: 6.6 Word origins

Defining chaos

Compare the definitions for 'chaos' from *A Table Alphabeticall* and Dr Johnson's *A Dictionary of the English Language* in the Student Book. Ask students to vote on which definition they find most helpful and give reasons for their choice. Use an online dictionary to explore some modern-day definitions of the term.

Resources

Student Book 3: Activity 7, page 147

Organizing a dictionary

Challenge students to suggest alternative approaches to organizing words in a dictionary by alphabetical order, e.g. by word class, by categories. Explore the advantages and disadvantages of the suggested approaches and discuss why alphabetical order was used.

Extra Time

Ask students to find out more about Samuel Johnson.

A Table Alphabeticall

Use the weblink below to explore an electronic version of *A Table Alphabeticall*. Assign students letters to investigate – identifying words where the Modern English spelling has changed.

Resources

Student Book 3: Activities 6a and 6b, page 146

Weblink: www.library.utoronto.ca/utel/ret/cawdrey/cawdrey0.html

New vocabulary

Ask students to suggest and provide definitions for new vocabulary that they use with their friends and others. Explore the influences behind the suggested vocabulary.

Resources

Student Book 3: Activities 2a and 2b, page 144

Vocabulary challenge

Ask students to select another word from *A Table Alphabeticall* and create a new dictionary definition for this in the style of Samuel Johnson's *A Dictionary of the English Language*. Discuss which style of definition students find most helpful and why.

Resources

Student Book 3: Activity 4, page 146

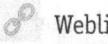 Weblink   Presentation   Interactive activity

Lesson focus

Why are we teaching this?

In this lesson, students will read a text that provides some advice on improving inflection in spoken contexts (in particular, when speaking on the telephone). Through discussion and role-play, they will also explore how to move between formal and informal registers in different contexts.

What are students learning?

Students will be able to:

- use inflection and intonation to actively involve a listener and communicate meaning
- understand how to move between formal and informal registers in different contexts.

How you could teach this

A variety of activities and approaches are provided on the right for you to select from and adapt to meet the needs of your students. The Kerboodle lesson player sequence is derived from these suggestions, to act as a starting point for your lesson.

Answers

Answers to Student Book activities, where relevant, can be found on page 153.

Teaching suggestions

Ignition

First telephone

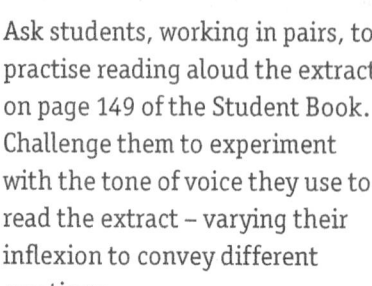

Show the 'Evolving design' image gallery on Kerboodle and ask students to identify the device being illustrated. Discuss how the design of the telephone has evolved in the nearly 150 years since its invention.

Resources

Kerboodle: 6.7 Evolving design 📷

Taking the call

Support Activity 1 in the Student Book by using the 'Taking the call' presentation on Kerboodle to ask students to role-play answering the telephone in a range of situations. Discuss the registers used in the different situations and encourage students to reflect on and discuss their language choices.

Resources

Student Book 3: Activity 1, page 148

Kerboodle: 6.7 Taking the call

Formal or informal

Use the 'Formal or informal' interactive activity on Kerboodle to allow students to use meaning and context clues to identify differences in formality.

Resources

Kerboodle: 6.7 Formal or informal 🖰

Exploration

Improving your inflexion

Ask students, working in pairs, to practise reading aloud the extract on page 149 of the Student Book. Challenge them to experiment with the tone of voice they use to read the extract – varying their inflexion to convey different emotions.

Prior experience

Ask students to reflect on the tone of voice they use when speaking on the telephone in different situations. Take examples and discuss how they alter their tone of voice, according to the situation in which they are speaking. Discuss how important tone of voice is for effective telephone communication.

Resources

Student Book 3: Activity 1, page 148

and guidance

Role-play

Ask students to role-play a phone call where a customer speaks to a mobile phone employee to complain about their mobile phone service. Ensure that students take turns in playing the role of the customer and the employee. Encourage them to take different approaches to each role – using the inflexion in their voice to suggest their emotions.

Resources
Student Book 3: Activity 2, page 148

Telephone conventions

Use the 'Telephone conventions' worksheet on Kerboodle to get students to explore the conventions governing telephone conversations in different countries and different contexts.

Resources
Kerboodle: 6.7 Telephone conventions

Discussion

Ask students to share their personal views about telephone etiquette. Pose questions such as: 'Is it rude to answer your phone when you are talking to your parents?'

Register

Use the 'Register' worksheet on Kerboodle to provide further support for students when completing Activity 3 in the Student Book.

Resources
Student Book 3: Activity 3, page 149

Kerboodle: 6.7 Register

Consolidation

Evaluation

Two stars and a wish: Ask students to decide on two things they did well when performing their role-play and one thing they could improve.

Resources
Student Book 3: Activity 2, page 148

Involving your listener

Ask students to create a list of their top three tips for involving a listener in a telephone conversation. Share tips and agree a class list of the top three.

Call centre

Discuss the skills needed to work in a call centre. Role-play a job interview for a person applying for such a position.

Extra Time

Ask students to write their own guide to mobile phone etiquette.

Lesson focus

Why are we teaching this?

In this lesson, students will read an extract from a live blog reporting on the birth of the Duke and Duchess of Cambridge's baby, as well as a newspaper report about the same event, in order to compare the language and structure of both forms. By discussing the advantages and disadvantages of live blogging, in comparison with traditional newspaper reports, students will also develop their understanding of how technological changes in the way people consume news, e.g. via the Internet (accessed increasingly via mobile devices), is affecting the conventions of the form.

What are students learning?

Students will be able to:

- compare the language and structure of live blogging with newspaper reports.

How you could teach this

A variety of activities and approaches are provided on the right for you to select from and adapt to meet the needs of your students. The Kerboodle lesson player sequence is derived from these suggestions, to act as a starting point for your lesson.

> **Answers**
>
> Answers to Student Book activities, where relevant, can be found on page 153.

Teaching suggestions

Ignition

Getting the news

Ask students to name the sources they use to find out what is happening in the news, e.g. reading a newspaper, online news sites, watching TV news bulletins, radio news bulletins, Twitter, etc. Rank the sources identified in order of popularity amongst students and frequency of use. Encourage students to identify the characteristics of the most-popular news source, e.g. radio news bulletin (highlights the top stories in brief, etc.)

Headlines

Display an online news website, such as BBC News. Discuss the headlines shown and identify any breaking news stories. Discuss students' expectations about the information they'll find out if they click through to the story behind the headline, and how it will be presented.

Resources
Weblink: www.bbc.co.uk/news/

Activate prior knowledge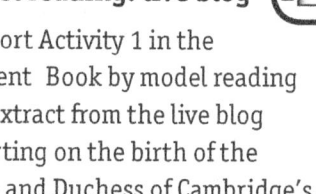

Ask students to explain what 'live blogging' is. Use the 'Live blogging' presentation on Kerboodle to ensure that students understand the conventions of the form and the range of news contexts in which live blogs can be used.

Resources
Kerboodle: 6.8 Live blogging

Exploration

Live bloggers

Use the 'Live blogging' worksheet on Kerboodle to enable students to activate and develop their knowledge of the conventions of the live blog form.

Resources
Kerboodle: 6.8 Live blogging

Model reading: live blog

Support Activity 1 in the Student Book by model reading the extract from the live blog reporting on the birth of the Duke and Duchess of Cambridge's baby. Identify how the text is structured (e.g. bite-sized updates provided over time); the style and formality of the language being used (e.g. the informal reference to 'Kate', and the conversational, jokey tone: 'Well, we can safely rule out one particular royal pilot being at the controls'); and the way in which information from other sources is referred to and included (e.g. embedded tweets, hyperlinks, etc.)

Resources
Student Book 3: Activity 1, page 150

Key for Kerboodle LRA resources Lesson Player Image Video Worksheet

and guidance

Consolidation

Model reading: newspaper report

Continue to support Activity 1 by model reading the extract from the newspaper report on the birth of the Duke and Duchess of Cambridge's baby. Identify how the text is structured (e.g. the introductory paragraph summarizing the key information, etc.); the style and formality of the language being used (e.g. the formal tone, the reference to 'The Duchess of Cambridge', etc.); and the way in which information from other sources has been referred to and included (e.g. direct quotations from the Kensington Palace statement).

Resources
Student Book 3: Activity 1, page 150

Discussion

Run Activity 2 in the Student Book as a whole-class discussion. Ask students to suggest the advantages and disadvantages of reading a live blog over a newspaper report from different perspectives, e.g. an office worker, a student, a retired person, etc. Encourage them to consider the different types of live blog that exist (e.g. breaking news blog, minute-by-minute football match blog, etc.) and the advantages and disadvantages these offer over other forms of media (e.g. TV news bulletins, live football, etc.)

Resources
Student Book 3: Activity 2, page 150

Breaking news!

Use the 'Breaking news!' image gallery on Kerboodle to role-play a breaking news story and ask students to live blog the events as they occur. Ensure that you display the images in sequence – allowing time for students to update their live blog with the latest event before introducing a new development.

Resources
Kerboodle: 6.8 Breaking news!

Who do you trust?

Display the 'Principles of journalism' presentation on Kerboodle. Discuss whether students think that journalism always lives up to these principles. Explore which format (live blog or traditional newspaper report) students think is more likely to be accurate in its reporting of the news. Take a class vote on how much students trust journalists to tell the truth. You could use the weblink below to compare the results of the class vote with a similar nationwide survey.

Resources
Kerboodle: 6.8 Principles of journalism

Weblink: www.prospectmagazine.co.uk/magazine/peter-kellner-yougov-trust-journalists/#.UmQu8XBwqRE

Journalism skills

Ask students to list the skills needed by a print journalist who writes traditional newspaper reports. Now ask them to list the skills needed by an online news blogger. Identify and discuss the skills in common and those specific to the role of an online news blogger.

Top tips

Ask students to agree a class list of top tips for writing a live blog.

Blog to report

Ask students to create their own live blog. This could be for a sporting event or a breaking news story.

Resources
Student Book 3: Activity 3, page 151

Extra Time

Ask students to transform their live blog from Activity 3 into a traditional newspaper report. Discuss the structural and stylistic changes they will need to make.

Lesson focus

Why are we teaching this?

This lesson will help to prepare students for the next lesson's end-of-unit assessment. It is based around a newspaper article, which presents interviews with three generations of the same family – all talking about their use of modern technology to communicate. Students then have to conduct their own interviews to explore the methods of communication used by their classmates.

What are students learning?

Students will be able to:

- explore the ways in which different generations use technology to enable communication.

How you could teach this

A variety of activities and approaches are provided on the right for you to select from and adapt to meet the needs of your students. The Kerboodle lesson player sequence is derived from these suggestions, to act as a starting point for your lesson.

Answers

Answers to Student Book activities, where relevant, can be found on page 153.

Teaching suggestions

Ignition

Letters of note

Ask students when they last wrote or received a letter (if ever) and discuss in which contexts they might consider sending one. Use the weblink below to explore examples of letters from the 'Letters of Note' website and use them to discuss the advantages and disadvantages of the form.

Resources

Weblink: www.lettersofnote.com/

Communication audit

Ask students to list the main methods of communication they use, and then rank order them in terms of popularity – from the most frequently used to the least frequently used. Take feedback and discuss the contexts in which different methods of communication tend to be used, e.g. texting friends, etc.

Online privacy

Display the statement: 'I wouldn't put anything online that I believe to be secret.' Discuss whether or not students agree with this statement – encouraging them to draw on their own experiences to support their views.

Resources

Student Book 3: Activity 2, page 152

Exploration

Shared reading

Use shared reading to identify the comments made by each generation of the family interviewed in the Student Book extracts to indicate their views about how different methods of communication affect both language use and behaviour, e.g. 'There are so many forms of communication now. I think this means people make last minute plans, or they make arrangements which they simply don't keep.'

Resources

Student Book 3: Activity 1, page 152

Spoken language

Use the weblink below to show the video presentation of a poem by Taylor Mali. Discuss whether students recognize any of the stylistic features of spoken language that the poet criticizes. Ask them to identify any features of spoken language that they find annoying themselves, and to create their own poem or presentation challenging these.

Resources

Weblink: www.thepoke.co.uk/2013/08/12/this-video-is-like-important/

Key for Kerboodle LRA resources Lesson Player Image Video 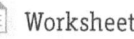 Worksheet

and guidance

Consolidation

Email formality

As a follow-up to Activity 4 in the Student Book, highlight Chloe Hamilton's comment on email formality from the extract on page 155. Discuss which email salutations and sign-offs students use, and explore the level of formality that they would use when emailing for different purposes, e.g. job application, thank you email to relative, etc.

Resources
Student Book 3: Activity 4, page 152

Ignite English interview

You might like to play Ignite Interview Film 2 to the class, in which Fiona McPherson discusses language and language change.

Resources
Kerboodle: 6 Ignite Interview Fiona McPherson Film 2

Interview skills

Use the 'Interview skills' worksheet on Kerboodle to help students to prepare for and complete Activity 5 in the Student Book.

Resources
Student Book 3: Activity 5, page 152

Kerboodle: 6.9 Interview skills

Social media overload

Ask students to discuss their use of social media, such as Facebook, Twitter, etc. Ascertain how often they use social media and for how long each day, and discuss how this affects them. You could ask students to debate this issue – selecting students to speak for and against the statement: 'Social media is too demanding'.

Extra Time

Ask students to interview different members of their family (e.g. parents, grandparents, younger/older siblings, etc.) to find out how they use technology to communicate and their views about this.

Summarizing

For each member of the family interviewed in the Student Book extracts, ask students to write a paragraph summarizing how they use technology to communicate and their views about it. You could assign different generations of the family to different groups of students.

Resources
Student Book 3: Activity 1, page 152

Sharing findings

Ask students to share their initial findings from the interviews they conducted in response to Activity 5 in the Student Book. Highlight any interesting points raised.

Resources
Student Book 3: Activity 5, page 152

Family communication

As a prelude or follow-up to the Extra Time activity, ask students to discuss how different members of their own family use technology to communicate. As a class, they could create a Venn diagram to show how the use of different communication methods overlaps the generations.

Assessment focus

Why are we assessing this?

This unit has developed students' spoken English and analytical skills. They have read a range of non-fiction extracts exploring how communications technology has changed language. This assessment now enables students to give a presentation to share their thoughts and views on this issue through the prism of how communications technology is used by teenagers.

What are students demonstrating?

Students will be able to:

- give a presentation, communicating ideas clearly and speaking fluently with appropriate tone, pace and intonation.

How to deliver the assessment

Suggestions and guidance on how to set up and prepare your students for the assessment are provided, as well as possible approaches to marking the assessment.

Alternative/additional assessment

There is an alternative end-of-unit assessment available on Kerboodle. This assessment leads to a writing outcome and can be used either in addition to or instead of the Student Book end-of-unit assessment.

Resources

Kerboodle: 6.10 Alternative end-of-unit assessment

Assessment suggestions and guidance

Understanding the assessment

Check that students understand the assessment task set. Emphasize that they are being tested on their *spoken* English skills and that they should draw on the skills and knowledge they have developed through the unit.

Resources

Student Book 3: pages 156–157

Preparing for the assessment

Allow students adequate space to rehearse their presentation. If possible, think about making use of a drama space or other areas where students can rehearse effectively. If students wish to make use of visual aids and images, allow them access to the resources needed to prepare these, but remind students that the focus of the assessment will be on their spoken English skills.

Completing the assessment

For students working in pairs or small groups, ensure that each role is large enough to provide evidence to enable a valid assessment of individual students' spoken English skills. If possible, film the presentations to collect evidence to support your assessment.

Timing and presentation expectation

Give students one hour (ideally one lesson) and expect a three to five-minute presentation.

Marking

You will want to mark this in line with departmental and school marking guidelines. If you wish, you could use the Ignite English marking scales provided on Kerboodle. Using the Ignite English marking scales will help you to identify specific strengths and areas for improvement in individual student's spoken English skills. This may help you to set development targets as well as build a profile of your class as speakers and presenters.

Refer to the KS3 National Curriculum and Ignite English mapping grids on pages 154–156 of this Teacher Companion to identify other Ignite English units where these spoken English skills are covered, or ask students to use the SPAG interactives on Kerboodle to address any areas identified for improvement. The Grammar Reference Guide on Kerboodle contains definitions and additional examples of each of the spelling, punctuation and grammar points covered in the interactives, for your reference.

Resources

Kerboodle: 6 Ignite English marking scales

Kerboodle: SPAG interactives

Kerboodle: Grammar Reference Guide

Worksheet   Interactive activity

Student Book answers

Below are the answers to any largely non-subjective Student Book activities contained within this unit.

Lesson 1

1   Students could identify the following details:
   - An over-reliance on computers/smartphones in the workplace.
   - The negative impact on writing skills.
   - The over-use of mobile phones and social media during working hours.
   - Young people lacking confidence/social skills in real-world situations.

Lesson 3

3a If you can read this you can get a good job with high pay.

3b Students could comment on how the sentence omits information (vowels and consonants), but the meaning is still understandable by the recipient.

Lesson 4

1   Students could pick out the following similarities:
   - The ability to transmit information rapidly over great distances.
   - The brevity of messages.

2   Students could identify the following techniques:
   - Dropping pronouns.
   - The use of abbreviations.
   - The use of code words.

Lesson 5

1   In the old days, when King Arthur ruled the land, England was still a magical land. I read that they believed that there were elves and fairies, and that the elf-queen herself could be seen dancing with other magical creatures in the forests. Now these creatures are gone and there are no more elves and fairies to be found anywhere.

Lesson 6

1a Influences behind new vocabulary:
   - Fashion: *flatform*, *geek chic*, *jorts*
   - Technology: *selfie*, *phablet* (*Selfie*: Hilary Clinton using the word in a text message to the owner of a Tumblr dedicated to images of her texting.)

KS3 National Curriculum and *Ignite English* mapping: **Reading**

	National Curriculum: subject content	Unit 1: Dare to Scare	Unit 2: Relationships	Unit 3: Exploring Difference	Unit 4: My Life, My Choices	Unit 5: Young Entrepreneurs	Unit 6: From Talking Drums to Tweets
Develop an appreciation and love of reading and read increasingly challenging material independently	Reading a wide range of fiction and non-fiction, including in particular whole books, short stories, poems and plays with a wide coverage of genres, historical periods, forms and authors. The range will include high-quality works from:		L3	L2, L3, L4	L2, L3, L4, L5, L6, L7, L8, L9	L1, L3, L4, L5, L8, L9	L1, L3, L4, L6, L7, L8, L9
	· English literature, both pre-1914 and contemporary, including prose, poetry and drama	L1, L2, L3, L4, L5, L6, L8, L9	L1, L2, L3, L4, L5, L6, L7, L8, L9	L6, L7, L8			L5
	· Shakespeare (two plays)	L7			L4 (TC)		
	· seminal world literature			L5			
	Choosing and reading books independently for challenge, interest and enjoyment	L9					
	Re-reading books encountered earlier to increase familiarity with them and provide a basis for making comparisons						
Understand increasingly challenging texts	Learning new vocabulary, relating it explicitly to known vocabulary and understanding it with the help of context and dictionaries	L3, L5 (TC)	L3	L7 (TC)	L5, L7, L8	L1, L3, L5	L5, L6
	Making inferences and referring to evidence in the text	L3, L4, L5	L1, L2, L4, L6, L7	L5, L6, L7, L8	L9	L1	
	Knowing the purpose, audience for and context of the writing and drawing on this knowledge to support comprehension	L7 (TC)	L4 (TC), L6, L9	L2, L7 (TC)	L4, L7, L9	L4, L5 (TC), L8	L5, L8
	Checking their understanding to make sure that what they have read makes sense	L3, L4, L5	L2, L4, L5, L9	L6, L7	L1, L6	L3, L8, L9	L1, L4, L5, L6, L9
Read critically	Knowing how language, including figurative language, vocabulary choice, grammar, text structure and organizational features, presents meaning	L1, L2, L3, L4, L5, L6, L8, L9	L1, L5, L7, L8	L2, L3, L4, L5, L6, L7, L8	L2, L3, L4, L5, L7, L8, L9	L9	L5, L8
	Recognizing a range of poetic conventions and understanding how these have been used	L5	L1, L2, L6, L7	L6			
	Studying setting, plot and characterization, and the effects of these	L1, L2, L3, L4, L5, L6, L9	L5, L8	L3, L6, L7, L8			
	Understanding how the work of dramatists is communicated effectively through performance and how alternative staging allows for different interpretations of a play	L7					
	Making critical comparisons across texts	L4, L6 (TC), L7 (TC), L9	L1 (TC), L2 (TC), L4 (TC), L9	L6			L6
	Studying a range of authors, including at least two authors in depth each year	L1, L2, L3, L4, L9	L1, L2, L3, L4, L5, L6, L7, L8, L9	L5, L6, L7			L5

KS3 National Curriculum and *Ignite English* mapping: **Writing**

National Curriculum: subject content	Unit 1: Dare to Scare	Unit 2: Relationships	Unit 3: Exploring Difference	Unit 4: My Life, My Choices	Unit 5: Young Entrepreneurs	Unit 6: From Talking Drums to Tweets
Writing for a wide range of purposes and audiences, including: • well-structured formal expository and narrative essays	L9		L8			
• stories, scripts, poetry and other imaginative writing	L1 (TC), L4 (TC), L5 (TC), L6, L8	L3 (TC), L6, L7, L9 (TC), L10	L3, L5, L6 (TC), L7 (TC)	L4		
• notes and polished scripts for talks and presentations			L4 (TC), L6	L4	L6, L9	
• a range of other narrative and non-narrative texts, including arguments, and personal and formal letters		L3 (TC), L8	L4, L6 (TC)	L2, L3, L5, L6, L8, L9, L10	L4, L6	L1 (TC), L2, L3, L7, L8
Summarizing and organizing material, and supporting ideas and arguments with any necessary factual detail	L5	L1	L2 (TC)	L1 (TC), L3 (TC), L7	L1, L6	L4, L9
Applying their growing knowledge of vocabulary, grammar and text structure to their writing and selecting the appropriate form	L1 (TC), L6, L8	L6, L10	L4, L5, L6 (TC)	L3, L4, L6, L8, L9, L10	L4, L5, L9	L3, L4, L8
Drawing on knowledge of literary and rhetorical devices from their reading and listening to enhance the impact of their writing	L6, L8	L6, L10	L3, L4, L6 (TC)			
Considering how their writing reflects the audiences and purposes for which it was intended	L6	L6, L10	L4	L2, L6, L10	L4, L6	L4
Amending the vocabulary, grammar and structure of their writing to improve its coherence and overall effectiveness	L6	L6, L10	L4	L2, L6, L10	L4, L6, L9	L4
Paying attention to accurate grammar, punctuation and spelling; applying the spelling patterns and rules set out in English Appendix 1 to the Key Stage 1 and 2 programmes of study for English	L6	L6 (TC), L10		L2, L10	L4, L9	

Write accurately, fluently, effectively and at length for pleasure and information

Plan, draft, edit and proofread

KS3 National Curriculum and *Ignite English* mapping: **Grammar and vocabulary**

National Curriculum: subject content	Unit 1: Dare to Scare	Unit 2: Relationships	Unit 3: Exploring Difference	Unit 4: My Life, My Choices	Unit 5: Young Entrepreneurs	Unit 6: From Talking Drums to Tweets
Extending and applying the grammatical knowledge set out in English Appendix 2 to the Key Stage 1 and 2 programmes of study to analyse more challenging texts	L2, L3, L4, L8	L5	L3, L7, L8	L2 (TC), L8, L9		L3
Studying the effectiveness and impact of the grammatical features of the texts they read	L2, L3, L4, L8		L3, L7, L8	L8, L9		
Drawing on new vocabulary and grammatical constructions from their reading and listening, and using these consciously in their writing and speech to achieve particular effects	L8		L3	L1, L8, L9	L9	L3, L8
Knowing and understanding the differences between spoken and written language, including differences associated with formal and informal registers, and between Standard English and other varieties of English	L8 (TC)	L5			L4, L9	L3, L7
Using Standard English confidently in their own writing and speech			L8	L1, L8	L4, L9	L2
Discussing reading, writing and spoken language with precise and confident use of linguistic and literary terminology	L2, L4, L8	L1, L5	L3, L7, L8		L4	L3, L7

Also available: A wealth of SPAG interactives on Kerboodle LRA 1, 2 and 3.

KS3 National Curriculum and *Ignite English* mapping: **Spoken English**

National Curriculum: subject content	Unit 1: Dare to Scare	Unit 2: Relationships	Unit 3: Exploring Difference	Unit 4: My Life, My Choices	Unit 5: Young Entrepreneurs	Unit 6: From Talking Drums to Tweets
Using Standard English confidently in a range of formal and informal contexts, including classroom discussion		L9	L1, L4 (TC), L5, L7 (TC)	L1	L2, L3	L1, L2, L5, L7, L8, L9
Giving short speeches and presentations, expressing their own ideas and keeping to the point			L1, L6	L1	L7, L10	L9
Participating in formal debates and structured discussions, summarizing and/or building on what has been said	L1 (TC), L5 (TC), L6 (TC)	L3	L1	L3 (TC)	L2, L3	
Improvising, rehearsing and performing play scripts and poetry in order to generate language and discuss language use and meaning, using role and intonation, tone, volume, mood, silence, stillness and action to add impact	L1 (TC), L3 (TC), L7	L2, L4	L6